CLARA M. CHANEY
N.C. Kephart Glen Haven Achievement Center

NANCY R. MILES
Educational Clinician and
Learning Disabilities Consultant

REMEDIATING LEARNING PROBLEMS:
A DEVELOPMENTAL CURRICULUM

CHARLES E. MERRILL PUBLISHING COMPANY
A Bell & Howell Company   *Columbus, Ohio*

THE SLOW LEARNER SERIES
Newell C. Kephart, Founding Editor

Published by
CHARLES E. MERRILL PUBLISHING COMPANY
A Bell & Howell Company
Columbus, Ohio 43216

Library of Congress Catalog Card Number: 73-92372

International Standard Book Number: 0-675-08816-X

2 3 4 5 6 7 8 9—78 77 76 75

Printed in the United States of America

To the late N.C. Kephart for his many years of teaching, encouragement, and inspiration by his judicious use of driving, coaxing, patience, humor, sharing, suggestion, insistence, questioning, guidance, and for his essential kindness and humanitarianism.

Preface

Interferences with development can occur at any stage of development (before birth, during birth or any time throughout life) and for any of a number of reasons, including neurological or sensory deficits, experiential deprivation, chemical imbalances, infantile allergies, nutritional deficiencies, and infections.

Remediation of such interferences involves:

1. Actively teaching the child what he failed to learn normally.

2. Helping the child through therapy to find a way around the deficit or through the protective halo the child has built around his deficit.

3. Altering the presentation of material so that it can be processed in terms of abilities which the child has avaliable to him through education.

4. Giving the child something that will permit him to perform in spite of the fact that he has a deficit (e.g., the use of a prothesis or crutch).

5. Avoiding a disturbance by the preventive provision of adequate stimulation for every child from birth on. Included in this aspect are attention to nutritional status and physiological chemistry of the organism from the earliest possible point.

The authors have been involved with research and training in the area of learning problems for fifteen years, first at Purdue University and later at the N.C. Kephart Glen Haven Achievement Center in Fort Collins, Colorado. Children admitted to this program have evidenced a myriad of learning problems, ranging from motor deficits to interferences on the academic level.

In the pages that follow, attention is directed to the development of all the senses, but emphasis is placed upon kinesthesia (awareness of movement). Particular emphasis is given to the motor development of the child because movement and motor exploration comprise the child's first encounter with his environment. It is on these first encounters that all future learning is built.

This book provides the reader with an understanding of the processes involved in learning. It discusses the results of breakdowns or deficiencies in these learning processes, and suggests remedial activities to overcome such difficulties.

CLARA M. CHANEY
NANCY R. MILES

Purpose of the Curriculum

This curriculum has been written for flexible use in aiding the professional or parent to teach children. It is not to be relegated to a specific group of children and may be used successfully with a broad range of children, including those who have learning disabilities, are retarded, are culturally deprived and fall within the so-called normal range.

Included in the last group may be the hypertensive child who has not yet evidenced learning disabilities. Special mention is made of him, for he can gain so much from the tasks listed herein. When used with the normal child, the curriculum will aid in identifying minimal interferences, or deficits, and thus serve a preventive purpose.

Children penalized by a learning disability will be approached through work on the interferences and deficits. Because the curriculum presents learning patterns that are basic to all other learning, academics should be de-emphasized at these levels until the perceptual-motor tasks have been accomplished.

Retarded children will move more slowly through the tasks in the curriculum but will benefit greatly from its presentation throughout their early school years. In fact, the basic program for the pre-school-aged retarded youngster should be built around the tasks presented on the following pages.

Finally, the curriculum will supply many experiences that the environment does not provide for the culturally deprived.

Instructions for Use of the Curriculum

Read aloud. It has been our experience that even with the author's best intentions, presentations of tasks are quite often misunderstood, or the speed reader skips pertinent words completely. Reading aloud the instructions or descriptions of a task to another person or to a child will sometimes help to clarify any ambiguity that may exist.

Perform. Unfortunately, there are times when the printed pages doesn't tell all, and there are people who need to *do* a task to understand its meaning. Therefore, performing the task before presenting it to the child will establish a standard of what to expect in terms of the youngster's performance. Keep in mind however, that these activities are for children who are or should be much more agile than most adults.

Experiment. Not all activities will work with all children. Therefore, use a task suggestion but vary it to meet the needs of a particular child or group of children. Don't hesitate to try original ideas, keeping in mind the goals which you are endeavoring to achieve.

Know the Curriculum. Read the entire curriculum before using it. A knowledge of what is presented will enable the instructor to work flexibly, to pinpoint the area in which to work, and to determine what methods are to be used or when to move forward or backward.

Application of the Curriculum.   After determining the level at which the child is operating, it will be necessary for you to observe why he is not operating efficiently.

You will find those children who are performing conceptually; that is, those who are using language, solving problems and so on, but who have by-passed motor-perceptual or perceptual-motor stages. These children will have no firm base for their concepts unless they develop good perceptual-motor generalizations and relate their concepts to them. Other children will be operating inefficiently at the motor-perceptual or perceptual-motor levels and, thus, will be having difficulty with perceptual-conceptual relationships.

Determination of Stage.   Through the use of tests (*Perceptual-Motor Survey, Frostig, ITPA, WISC, Stanford-Binet,* etc.) and checklists, such as "Motoric Aids to Perceptual Training," "Ready or Not," etc., and empirical observations (at home, on playground, in classroom), a preliminary decision may be made regarding the stage of development of a given child and the level or levels on which he is performing. The child's abilities and needs also must be taken into consideration.

After this determination has been made, check back to a previous stage to see if reinforcement is needed to help him perform more adequately. If the child at a certain stage (i.e., perceptual) is performing some of the appropriate tasks but not others, then move back to a previous stage (perceptual-motor) to see what is interfering in his progress.

It will be better for the student to start on a low level and experience success than to start at too-high a level and continue to experience the frustration and failure that has been his companion—sometimes for many years.

Checklist.   After the administration of the indicated evaluative instruments, the child's performance level may be charted upon the checklist.

Lesson Plan.   A lesson plan is suggested to aid persons in contact with the child to:

1. Become keen observers of a child's behavior.
2. Know day by day or week by week what has been done, how and what were the results obtained.

Such records prove invaluable in scheduling, for research, and for parent conferences as well as for self-evaluation by the teacher in reference to her program and its success.

Projection Sheet. The projection sheet may be used for both initial and subsequent evaluations and to organize and order the tasks recommended for remediation. This format will help the teacher to think in terms of the goals of the program: "Why have you presented these tasks?" Should the projected goals not be obtained, the teacher should ask herself:

1. "Were the goals realistic in terms of the child's functioning?"
2. "Were the tasks presented realistically in terms of the way the child processes information?"
3. "Was attention geared to the product or end result rather than the process?"
4. "Has positive reinforcement been used for every small success?" ("Small success" means any real attempt by the child to solve his problem.) Too often successful completion of or attempts at a task are reinforced in terms of a teacher's goal rather than the child's.

Outline of Pre-Readiness

GOAL

Development of: Body image (i.e., body form, space, and time); Internal language; Speech.

MECHANICS WITH WHICH THE CHILD IS BORN

Reflexive movement; Global movement; Sensory receptors.

KEYS TO LEARNING

Movement with attention to kinesthesia (i.e., internal input or stimuli); Attention to external input or stimuli (i.e., visual, tactual, and auditory stimuli).

SKILLS TO BE LEARNED

MOVEMENTS

Reflexive: Integration—chaining, tying, conditioning.

De-emphasis of: Dependence on reflex action through development of purposeful of controlled movements.

Purposeful Motor Differentiation: Mechanism of body, eyes, and speech; Kinesthetic figure-ground; Isolation of muscles and joints; Movement control; Automation.

Coordination: Semi-mechanical, mechanical, synchronous.

SENSORY PERCEPTIONS

Sensory attention, differention, perceptual location of figure-ground, and isolation.

Pre-readiness Learning Culminates in the Development of: Motor-perceptual match—kinesthetic-kinesthetic, kinesthetic-visual, kinesthetic-auditory; Motor-perceptual generalizations—balance, contact (reach, grasp, release), locomotion, receipt, and propulsion; Body image—elemental form, space, and time—parts, movements, functions, movement *vs* non-movement, hereness-nowness; Associated form—parts related to the whole, parts related to the parts; Internal language—jargon; Speech—imitation; Language—gestures, first words.

As the child's movements become automatic and he no longer needs to attend to and direct them, he shifts his attention from self-movement to end results—from self to the environment. He can then develop percepts about the things he moves and manipulates and verify new percepts through movement and manipulation. Through systematic exploration, he will make new discoveries and learn the terms to name, define, and describe them. In other words, he enters the world of Readiness.

In the process, he will advance through three stages, accumulate and elaborate new information in each stage, and integrate it with previous information. These stages are: Motor-perceptual—motor exploration with perceptual observation; Perceptual-motor—perceptual exploration with motor verification; Perceptual—perceptual exploration with perceptual verification.

Outline of Readiness

An outline of Readiness Learning and Section One of the Readiness Curriculum are included in this volume to help the reader with transition into the readiness period. The remainder of the material that has been developed on readiness was not included because of the need to place emphasis on the importance of pre-readiness preparation and in order to prevent the presentation of readiness material before the tools of learning (i.e., the child's own body) have developed.

GOAL

To help the child to interact with and to learn from his immediate environment; in other words, to help the child to orient himself in the environment; relate and associate objects, actions, and events within it; learn its language and inter-relate self, environment, and language.

PRE-READINESS ABILITIES NEEDED

Coordination, automatic movements, motor-perceptual match, motor-perceptual generalizations, body image, speech and gestures, language.

KEYS TO LEARNING

Systematic exploration.

SKILLS TO BE LEARNED

Functional use of large- and small-muscle groups; Perceptual-motor match; Orientation of self in environment; Relationships of elements within that environment.

As the child becomes comfortably established in his environment, he ventures deeper into it to explore and experiment with its finer details. He enters the second, or pre-academic, phase of Readiness and uses his knowledge of self and environmental form, space, and time to:

A. Reproduce:

   1. With building materials:

      a. That which he has explored or experienced.
      b. That which he sees.

   2. With a writing tool:

      a. His own movements.
      b. That which he sees.

B. Identify, organize, and integrate printed symbols.

The child's success will depend upon how systematically he has gathered and integrated information regarding his objective world and the speech symbols.

Readiness activities should be presented sequentially as:

1. Perceptual-motor tasks (i.e., tasks presented perceptually with materials that can be explored motorically for verification).

2. Perceptual tasks (i.e., tasks presented perceptually with perceptual matching and verification).

Readiness Learning Culminates in: Constructive form (objective and symbolic); Organization of space; Organization of time; and Development of social language.

Contents

part 1

Pre-Readiness: First Level—

Becoming Aware of Movement

chapter 1

Body Movement and Speech

MOVEMENT AND SENSORY AWARENESS

The first movements a child makes are accidental, caused by others or by reflex impulses. The child moves, sees, hears and feels. Occasionally, he realizes he is moving or receiving sensory stimuli. When he does so he attends totally. Thus, if he becomes aware of his movements he ceases to see, hear or feel, unless a strong stimulus is presented, over time, to attract his attention. The moment he attends visually or auditorily he ceases to move, because the movement now becomes the lesser stimulus. After many such experiences he finds that he can repeat the acts of looking, listening and moving and that they are separate tasks even though he is totally involved in each.

A few school age children with learning disabilities need some reinforcement at this level. As a rule, deficits are not noted in more than one of the above areas (except for the severely involved or cerebral palsied).

Training involves making the child aware that he can and does move and that he can and does use his senses as receptors.

MOVEMENT

If the child cannot make simple head, arm or leg movements on command or in imitation, yet you see him making them in acts of daily living, he should be made aware of his ability to move. Since he will need to give his full attention to the movement, profuse visual or auditory clues that will distract him from the assigned task should be avoid-

3

ed. Keep verbalization (adult's and child's) and other distracting sounds to a minimum. If there are things in the room that distract the child visually, clear the area or use a blindfold.

In the tasks described below, the child should lie on the floor or sit in a semi-reclined position. Use tactual-kinesthetic cues to call the child's attention to the part to be moved; deep pressure, rubbing, or shaking are effective.

Manipulation: Tell the child what part of him you are going to move and then move it two or three times. As soon as you stop, tell him to move it.

Prodding: You may need to prod and poke to get the movement started and continue prodding to keep it moving.

Uncomfortable Positioning: If, after several attempts, the above procedure does not get results, place the child's limb or head in an uncomfortable position and hold it there until the child tires of the position and initiates a movement in the opposite direction. The moment he does so, release your hold, encourage him and prod to keep the movement going.

Example: With the child on his back on the floor, turn his head to the far right and then to the far left. Repeat several times. Then hold it in the far left position until the child tires of it there and initiates movement in the other direction. Make sure, however, that it is the movement you want. If you are working for head turning from side to side and the child rolls his body instead, he does not learn that he can turn his head. It is wise, therefore, to hold the body in place at the same time that the head is being turned.

Reflexive Tug: If it is a limb that is to be moved, place the limb in the opposing position then give a short, quick pull, setting off the "reflexive urge" to move in the opposite direction.

Example: If an upward movement is desired, give a quick tug downward; when the child makes a move in the right direction convey to him by a nod, smile or a few words that he performed correctly.

While performing the activities below, the child should lie on his back on the floor.

1. Raise an arm above his head and tug until the child initiates movement in the opposite direction. For some children short quick tugs are most effective. Others respond better to a steady strong pull.

2. Pull the child's arms straight up in the air and follow through as above.
3. Slide the child's leg out to the side
4. Grasp the heel of one foot and push the knee up lightly against the child's chest.

As soon as the child can move with minimal clues, introduce the head, arm and leg differentiation of the next stage.

NON-MOVEMENT

Many children fail to learn because they are never still long enough to attend to any kind of stimuli; they are always moving. Such a child must learn the art of relaxed non-movement. In the beginning you might find that one second is as long as a child can remain immobile and silent. During that second you can present the stimulus. The goal is to increase the periods of repose.

1. Help the child assume a relaxed position on his back, stomach and on each side. Begin with a count of two and work until he can maintain the position for a slow count up to fifteen.
2. Have the child do a lazy relaxed roll from one position to the other using arm, leg and the head to direct the roll rather than rigid trunk movements.

AUDITORY-VISUAL ATTENTION

If the child does not fixate, hold fixations or pursue *visual* and *auditory* stimuli, activities to help him develop these abilities should be introduced. However, auditory and visual training should be done separately. Use stimuli that give strong, clear visual or auditory clues. Bells, rattles, marracas, tambourines, a spoon in a cup, and so on, all make adequate auditory stimuli. Visual stimuli should be bright in color and should rotate or be shaken. Auditory fixations are marked by alert attentiveness—the child may cock his head. If a child is attending to visual stimuli he will perform as mentioned below. If not, he may have to be encouraged to perform in the following sequence:

1. Fixations: These occur in several ways: momentarily; over time; through slow movement of his eyes and his head from one object to another; while touching or grasping the stimulus object. (He should be able to make fixations without involving his hands.)
2. Pursuits of a moving target: At this stage visual pursuits are a series

of fixations and the target is easily lost. The child turns his head
with the movement of the target. The child indicates auditory pursuit by turning his head in the direction of the sound of the target.
His eyes do not need to attend to the target.

3.   Feel for tactual clues: Supply a variety of rough and smooth, soft
and hard objects for the child's experimentation. It is not necessary
for vision always to be involved since identification of the differences
is not necessary. The goal of the task is to make the child aware
that he can "feel" things.

VISUAL-MOTOR (TACTUAL-KINESTHETIC-VISUAL)

Exploration of hands: Encourage the child to look at his hands as
he moves his fingers and hands individually and separately. Put honey or
syrup on the child's hands and encourage him to stick his hands together
then pull them apart. Next he may put his fingers together and then
separate. The stickiness will enhance tactual awareness and draw the
eyes to the task. Finally, have him wash his hands until no stickiness is
left.

PREPARATION FOR SPEECH

In the beginning the child learns to suck, swallow, breathe and
exercise his speech mechanism by crying. Many children with delayed
speech have not yet learned to perform the above acts in a normal way.
They cannot suck adequately; to swallow they gulp, and their breathing
patterns are shallow or irregular. As long as a child must consciously
attend to these acts he cannot concentrate fully on speaking.

Early speech sounds are the result of practiced mouth movements.
The child, however, does not concentrate on the sound until the movement is well established. He is working too hard at moving to concentrate on the incidental results.

If the child needs help in elaborating his breathing, sucking and
swallowing patterns, the emphasis should be put on the movement
rather than on the sounds. The teacher should call the child's attention
to what his mouth is doing rather than the sound he is making. He may
also need to help the child position his mouth, tongue and lips.

PATTERNS

1.   Short inhalations—short exhalations: Each of the following will

produce a different sound (ehs, ahs, grunts, etc.): with the mouth wide open; with the mouth partially open; with the lips closed, breathing through the nose.

2. Short inhalations—long exhalations: Use pretend crying, pretend or real laughing, squealing.

3. Long inhalations—long exhalations: These include sighs, extended sounds (ah-ha, oh-ho, etc.), breathing through the mouth, breathing through the nose.

RELAXATION

Often a child's inadequate breathing and lack of speech result from excessive body tension, particularly in the abdomen, chest, neck and jaw. When this is the case, work for relaxation of these areas, simultaneously with the breathing.

Experiment with a variety of positions until you find the one in which the child's abdomen, chest and neck are most relaxed. We have found that the relaxation can often be accomplished by placing the child in one of the following positions:

1. Seated on the floor in a semi-supine position against another person. The adult should support the child with one of his arms, leaving the other free to manipulate and massage any part of the child's upper and lower torso in which tension might develop. It may also help to have the child's knees flexed and his legs apart. While in this position, they may be supported by the extended legs of the person behind him or by pillows.

2. Seated on the floor with his legs crossed "Indian fashion" with the upper torso relaxed and slightly slumped forward.

3. If the child is not relaxed in any of the above positions, then the tension in the abdomen, chest, neck and jaw will have to be alleviated through specific manipulation (see page 15).

Place the child in the semi-supine position as above or kneel in front of him. Relax the abdomen by placing a hand on either side of the stomach and gently massage until the stomach muscles relax. While the abdomen is stabilized in this manner, ask the child to perform the breathing activities. If necessary, turn the head to one side or tilt it back to release the tension in the neck and jaw muscles. If the neck and jaw muscles tighten as the child works, massage the neck muscles and manipulate the jaw until they relax; then continue. Should the above not help the child, refer to page 15.

SUCKING AND SWALLOWING

1.   In severe cases it may be necessary to make a game of sucking
     from a nippled bottle. Talk about feeding lambs or other small
     animals who have lost their mother. Introduce a pop bottle with a
     nipple on it and let the child try it out.
           Have the child try to suck and swallow while in many positions.
     Discourage thrusting of tongue out over lower teeth and lip while
     sucking. (While infantile sucking uses the tip of the tongue to press
     against nipple, the child learns later to use pressure and pull of lips,
     as tongue retracts in sucking).
2.   Have the child suck on (not bite) a stick of candy, long narrow ice
     cube, Popsicle, etc.
3.   Stress a suck-swallow sequence: Present him with the candy; he
     sucks it. Remove it and encourage swallowing (his lips may have
     to be held).

MOUTH MOVEMENTS

     Show the child how to:

1.   Tuck his tongue behind his lower teeth, inhale, then thrust the air
     outward to make the "k"and"g" sound.
2.   Repeatedly open and shut his mouth. Keep him relaxed as he works.

part 2

Pre-Readiness: Second Level

Learning to Move and to Control Movement and Behavioral Responses

chapter 2

Learning to Control Movement

CONTROL

A child's only means of making contact with his environment and of learning from it is through body movements and the information he receives from his eyes, ears, touch, etc. Movement plays a part in everything a child learns. For example, he moves his eyes to collect visual information or turns his head towards a sound. He also expresses his first needs, feelings and thoughts through movement.

It is important, therefore, that the child learn to sort out the many movements available to him. He must also learn to control them—make them do as he commands—before he can be expected to combine and integrate them in coordinated movements (visual-motor tasks, walking and so on). If his movements are restricted or uncontrolled, his education will also be restricted and disorganized.

Once the child learns to sort out his movements, coordinate and control them, he will be better able to control all of his responses, both social and educational. He will find it easier to adapt to the environmental demands of the home, school and community. The child who had difficulty initiating movement will no longer need to avoid or resist playing games with the other children, and he will become less withdrawn and resistive in the classroom.

Perseverative movements and activities will diminish as the child develops a greater repertory of controlled movements. The child who had been accused of shoving, striking out, and other careless or "aggressive" movements will be less careless or aggressive as he learns to control the termination of his movements (as he learns to stop.)

The child who has dashed through life creating havoc as he moved from one point to another will be less clumsy, destructive and hyperactive as he learns to control his movements from beginning to end. With control he will find it easier to learn and, consequently, will be easier to teach. Living with him will become more enjoyable.

DEFICITS

Children with movement deficits are not molded into a single pattern. They acquire their deficits by varied routes, and remediation should be designed accordingly.

One child may never have sorted out all the parts of his body and he either does not use them or he must activiate large sections of his body in order to incorporate them into an activity. Hyperkinesia develops and if it becomes severe enough it interferes with previously differentiated movements. It will be necessary to stress differentiation, then movement out of relaxation, and control, in teaching this child.

Another child may have differentiated his body parts as an infant, but met with difficulty when required to learn to make balancing adjustments in order to sit, stand, and walk. He might tense a few muscles in order to maintain the upright position, thus developing a rigid balancing pattern. The tension and rigid balance further limit the number and extent of differentiated movements. This child's problem is readily diagnosed; differentiation will come quickly if balance is not required while performing. Balance and movement out of relaxation will be factors during the training.

A third child may move with little or no awareness of his movements or the moving parts. He has differentiated his body parts, but has little if any awareness of how he moves, either through kinesthetic or visual awareness. Activity occurs; he does things, but has no memory of how he performed and therefore cannot repeat them. Although he appears to be elaborating his activities, he is incapable of duplications. He must be taught to attend to his movements kinesthetically, visually, auditorily and tactually. The greatest amount of emphasis should be upon kinesthetic awareness.

A fourth child may be hypotonic (always loose). He developed just enough differentiation and control to get by. Both movement and learning are limited in moderate to severe degrees. Movement against resistance to develop tonus and movement control is indicated; if tension develops during the activity, help the child learn to move the part out of relaxation, after he has differentiated it.

Finally, there may be the child who developed normally until the time that society demanded he perform activities for which he was not developmentally ready. The *overplaced* child is found in every classroom including kindergarten. He develops splintered movements (movements not related to his integrated body of movements). Body tension develops which will interfere with the previously learned movements. The child, for instance, who "chokes" his pencil in his attempt to write is using splintered finger movements during writing. Another child may not be visually ready for reading. This child needs to be placed at a grade level where he can take part in the assigned activities and experience success. The tasks that forced him to develop "splintered skills" should be eliminated or simplified. Others that will encourage the necessary differentiation, coordination, and control should be introduced. Relaxation techniques should be used to eliminate tension.

Some body tension is necessary when the child is learning to differentiate his body parts but it should disappear when the movement is learned. A body part is differentiated when the child can move it without overflow of movement into other parts and without tensing the moving part of other body parts. Differentiation must be present before the child can relax (unless he is securely supported). To relax a child's undifferentiated body may cause him to lose control of his body parts. It is usually easier to teach differentiation from the top to bottom (cephalo-caudal) and the inside to out (proximo-distal) directions.

Relaxation and movements out of relaxation are accomplished more easily in the reverse, from the extremities inward, but only those parts that are differentiated can move out of relaxation. After the child can make a differentiated movement out of relaxation, he may still need to isolate the various movements kinesthetically before he will be able to control his movements. Movement control is a pre-requisite for behavior control.

The hypertense child moves rigidly and rapidly. There seems to be no period of repose. All muslces in his body become taut during the simplest movements. When moving an individual body part, tension may be apparent in any other body part. These children are depicted in the literature as having a poor kinesthetic figure-ground. According to Kephart (1968) "the pattern of muscles required to perform a given movement stands out over the pattern of the remaining musculature.

The figure (the muscles required to perform) stands out in contrast to the ground (the remaining musculature)."[1] In this child, there is no contrast between ground and figures, as all muscles are stimulated to the maximum for movement.

Many children with learning disabilities have not developed a kinesthetic figure-ground that is strong enough to enable them to make the necessary comparisons between perceptual data and response data. "They have difficulty sorting out a particular response purposefully related to the perceptual data." (Kephart 1968).[2] These children may best be taught kinesthetic figure-ground through relaxation. Through the use of these techniques based upon Jacobsen's "Progressive Relaxation" the child is taught the following:

1. To become more aware of movement.
2. To develop motor coordination and coordination between perceptual data and motor data.
3. To learn to move efficiently through interactions of relaxation and contraction.
4. To learn to control his movements more adequately (tension interferes with movement control resulting in inconsistent, jerky motion).

The classroom teacher may be aware of youngsters who grasp their pencils tightly with stiff and inflexible fingers. Their wrist and elbow movements may be similar to those of the fingers. Writing tasks will be laboriously performed by these children. There will be other children whose neck and face muscles are so tight that they interfere with movement of the head and the information-gathering movements of the eyes. All teachers have had experience with youngsters who complain of stomachaches, headaches or those who "freeze" during a test. These quite often are the result of hypertension.

Many reasons are apparent for so much tension among the classroom population. Some of the children brought it with them; for others the effort of monitoring a task may be so great as to cause tension to occur in their necks, faces, and/or shoulders. For the same reason, lengthy tasks many times create tension and result in fatigue. If the child is required to work above his performance level, the frustration of inadequate preparation and repeated failures causes tension.

---

[1] "The Pattern of Muscles Required to Perform a Given Movement Stands Out over the Remaining Musculature." Unpublished lecture delivered at Glen Haven Achievement Center, Fort Collins, Colorado, 1968.

[2] *Ibid.*

RELAXATION

PROCEDURE

1. The teacher may work with the children as a group, or the children may take turns helping each other in the classroom or gym.
2. Each child should observe his body parts as they are moved. If this proves difficult or if tension persists, have them look at a designated visual target across the room (a drawing, a ball, book, etc.). Should tension still exist in some of the children, try blindfolding or having them close their eyes so that they receive only tactual-kinesthetic information and can give it their full attention. (Sometimes the information they receive from their eyes conflicts with that from movements, thus creating confusion and additional tension.)

   Use words that the children will understand. ("Loose, be like sphagetti, noodles, jello.") Tell them when they are loose and when they are tight, so they will learn to recognize the difference between the two.

   Not all children will need to work through the entire relaxation sequence. Some children will need only arms or legs, others the shoulders and neck. Fifteen minutes should be enough time for most school-age children to benefit from the overall approach of "working relaxed."

   Any of the therapy techniques may be recommended to parents by the teacher. These relaxation tasks may be performed at home with the parents helping, two or three times a day, five to ten minutes each time.

Relaxation of Stomach, Neck and Face

1. The child should be seated in a semi-supine position, between the legs of another person. His legs and shoulders should be relaxed.
   a. The person behind him is to use a continuous deep massage across the stomach muscles to relax them.
   b. If necessary, a second person may relax the right arm by massaging the area between the child's neck and his shoulder. Occasionally, gently shake the right arm to see if it looks and feels "loose."
   c. Ask the child to turn his head to the left. Massage any muscles that begin to tighten.
   d. The child's head rests in the turned position until the second therapist relaxes the left arm. Next ask the child to turn his head to the right. The tension is alleviated by the therapists.

e. Repeat the tasks on page 15 in each direction five or six times.
f. Continue until the child can turn his head without tensing other parts of his body.

2. *Breathing:* The child should breathe normally and rhythmically with his stomach muscles relaxed. If he has difficulty doing so refer to "Stomach Relaxation" and "Rhythmic Breathing" (Preparation for Speech), pages 3 and 4.

3. Ask the child to speak as he remains relaxed. He may count, say the ABC's, repetitious sounds, nursery rhymes, etc. The verbalization must be something that the child knows well. During these tasks if any tension is observed in the face, jaws, neck, and stomach, eliminate it by the methods above.

Movement of Limbs out of Relaxation

Goal: To reduce tension in the muscles not directly involved in the movement (the ground).

Observations: Based on above. Be aware of the other body parts. Even though they may not appear to be directly involved in the movement required, they must be kept relaxed to achieve the goal (i.e., observe neck, face, hands, toes, abdomen, etc. as you move the foot or leg).

1. Foot and Leg

a. The child assumes a semi-supine position against a back rest, pillows or another person (a person is best when a high degrees of tension is present).
b. Work from toes upward in most cases.
c. If tension is not present in the toes, work may be started at the ankle, calf, knee or thigh, or it may at times be necessary to relax the calf and thigh before the toes will relax.

(1) Manipulate the toes by moving them slowly back and forth with the palm of the hand. Work with each foot separately.
(2) To loosen the ankles, grasp the foot gently on either side of the arch and move it from side to side.
(3) Stabilize the ankle by holding and move the foot fore and aft, then in a circular movement (movement will be more restricted in this direction). Try these tasks on yourself to determine the realistic range of motion. Work slowly and gently. Work with each ankle separately.
(4) Flex the child's leg by lifting gently at the knee and move the knee slightly out to the side as it is raised; the foot slides along the floor. When sliding the foot on the floor rest the

heel on paper to reduce friction. When working on carpet rest heel on foil, small foil pans, or glass furniture cups to reduce friction.

Hold leg in flexed position, manipulate calf to be sure it is relaxed. Lower it to rest beside the other leg. Repeat with the opposite leg.

(5) Relaxation of the thigh may be obtained by placing a hand under the thigh muscle just above the knee, and with quick gentle up and down movements of the fingers (as a unit) loosen the muscles. Lift the leg slightly by flexing the knee, if necessary for relaxation. If tendons are tight, massage deeply across them with the hand flat until they loosen. In some cases the child must be on his stomach to achieve maximum release of tightness in this area (see Kinesthetic Awareness in this section). If adomen is tense, hold tightly with hands placed at an angle at either side of it. While stabilized in this manner have the child move his legs apart and together or up and down, singly and together. Massage of this area will also help to loosen the muscles.

As each body part relaxes have the child move it himself, slowly and easily, maintaining the relaxation. At first he may be able to make only one or two movements before becoming tight. If he tenses, stop the movement, re-establish relaxation, then proceed. (If, as he makes the movement, he uses the wrong muscle groups or over-uses the tendons and his performance cannot be corrected through relaxation, go immediately to Section III-Kinesthetic Awareness). Ask for movement of single parts and paired parts—rotate an ankle, both ankles, slide one leg out and back, slide both legs apart and together and so on.

If the child has more difficulty with one leg than the other, give additional time to the movement of that limb so that when he is required to move both simultaneously the movements will be coordinated and synchronous.

2. Arm and Hand

a. The child assumes a semi-supine position with his arm resting in a slightly flexed position.

(1) Fingers: Gently manipulate the fingers of each hand separately until the tension releases. Then have him move his fingers and open and shut his hand, keeping relaxed. Should tension occur in either hand repeat.

(2) Wrists: Manipulate the wrist, as the ankles, in an up and down, side to side and rotating movement. Shake the wrist gently.

The child then moves his wrist in the same manner. Should tension occur repeat.

(3) *Elbows.* Move the child's lower arm up and down bending the arm at the elbow. When he is relaxed, have the child move his arm.

(4) *Whole arm.* Lift up the whole arm slowly by the wrist shaking it gently as it moves. Let it drop onto a pillow or into someone's hand. Should it not drop, loosen by shaking and repeat. The child then repeats the task himself.

(5) Repeat the above procedures in the opposite arm.

MAKING RELAXATION MEANINGFUL

The relaxation now must be made meaningful in terms of the child's functioning, if he is to learn to apply it to everyday life. Therefore, when relaxation and movement out of relaxation of the child's body parts has been obtained through the teacher's or another child's manipulations, he should repeat them by himself.

The child may work with or without a blindfold during these tasks. A blindfold is recommended if optimum kinesthetic feedback is desired. It may also be used if it appears that vision constitutues an interference with movement or if tension is increased by the use of vision.

The following are the variations of movements to be used directly following the basic relaxation tasks:

1. The teacher moves the arm while maintaining relaxation.
2. The child is asked to repeat the same movement with the same part.
3. The child is asked to repeat the same movement with the opposite part.
4. For the child who has been working blindfolded, remove the blindfold and have him make the movement again as he watches.
5. The teacher makes two or more movements with the arm, e.g., flexion and extension of arm plus rotation of the forearm.
6. The child repeats 1. and 2. in this list in the same sequence as the teacher.
7. The teacher asks the child to change the order or to repeat the movement with the opposite limb first.

If the child can relax but continues to have difficulty moving a part without overflow movement or tension in other parts or if he persists in using the wrong muscle groups it is an indication that he has not differentiated parts of his body or has not developed kinesthetic isolation of the various muscle groups and joints. If this is the case, move on to the differentiation and isolation activities returning to movement out of relaxation as soon as the part is differentiated and/or isolated.

DIFFERENTIATION

These are additional differentiated movements that may need to be learned. Emphasize movement out of relaxation and call attention to the muscle groups the child is to use.

Differentiation of Neck and Hand

1. The child should lie on the floor on his stomach with his legs extended, arms flexed and his chin on the floor.

    a. He is to turn his head to the right, relax, then turn it back to the mid position and relax. In this task, and in all of the following tasks of differentiation, help him eliminate tension in other parts of the body by using deep massage, shaking or changing the position of the tense parts. Deep massage is done by using the flat of the hand to press firmly on tense muscle or tendon as the hand moves back and forth or in a rotary motion. Overflow movements can be eliminated by holding any part that moves, by interference (i.e., place the child so that the overflow movement will cause the limb to come in contact with an immovable object, block, board, brick, etc.) or through verbal reminders.

    b. The child turns his head to the left; let him relax, then turn it back to the mid position and again he is to relax.

    c. Have the child lie with the side of his face on the floor, then turn his head until the opposite side of the face is on the floor. He is to move his head in each direction.

       The child is to assume the same position as in a., then lift his head up, thrusting the chin forward. The chin should be only one half to one inch off the floor. The movement should be in the neck, not in the shoulders.

    e. Next have him lift his head and his shoulders and turn his head to look about.

2. The child now lies on his back on the floor, arms and legs extended with his face pointed toward the ceiling.

    a. He is to move his head from center to side while lying on his back, and from side to side.

    b. He is to lift his head off the floor, moving his chin down toward his chest as he does so. His shoulders should remain flat on the floor and relaxed. This may be a difficult movement for many children. If a child cannot perform, begin working with him in a semi-supine position, supported by a wedge of pillows, back rest, or if necessary by another person sitting behind him. Repeat each of the above task three to five times each training session, until the child can perform without tension and overflow.

Arm and Leg Differentiation (Tactual-Kinesthetic)

1. The child should lie on his stomach on the floor with his arms at his sides and legs extended downward.

   a. He is to slide his hand up along and near the side of his body. He is to continue to move until his arm is fully extended over his head. He then is to relax the hand, arm and body. Next have him slide the hand back down to the starting position. The child's head may be turned toward the moving arm or away from it. Repeat with each arm.

   b. He is to slide his knee up along the floor. His foot should move up along the floor near the opposite leg. When his knee is up as far as it will go easily, he is to relax, then slide it back down. The child may lie with both elbows flexed, or with the elbow flexed on the same side as the moving leg, the other arm straight. His face should be turned towards the side which is being moved. Possible positions:

   c. He is to lift a leg, raising the foot three inches from the floor, hold, then lower, keeping the knee straight throughout the task. The child should learn to hold to a slow count of five. If the child cannot keep his knee straight, hold it until he gets the feel of lifting from the hips. If that does not suffice, put a splint on his leg. A simple splint may be made by wrapping a magazine or thick newspaper around the knee. Secure it with straps, string, tape, etc.

2. The child is to lie on his back on the floor, his arms at his sides and his legs extended downward.

   He is to draw his knee up to his chest as you gently pull on his heel, relax, then return his leg to the floor while you gently resist it by pushing on his heel.

   b. He is to lift an arm from his side up over his head until it lies on the floor, relax, then lower it to his side. If he has difficulty keeping the elbow straight use a splint as in c. above.

   c. Raise his fore arm at right angles to his body. He is then to push upward against another's hand (or against a weight in his hand) until the arm is fully extended above his body. Next he is to pull downward until the elbow and the upper arm rest on the floor close to his torso.

   d. He is to lift a straight leg until the foot is five to eight inches off the floor, hold and then lower. Use a splint if necessary.

Repeat each of the activities above three to five times in succession. Perform each task with each limb, separately, unless otherwise specified. If the performance of one limb is repeatedly less adequate than the other, emphasize the activity for that limb.

Hip Differentiation

Should a child's hips be tight or tense or if the muscles at the side of the waist are too tense, it is well to precede the following tasks for "Kinesthesis and Control" with "Relaxation of Hips." Tension within the hip area will interfere with the goal of the task: awareness of movement.

1. The child should be blindfolded and should lie on his back on the floor.
2. Stand astride the child, place one hand on either side of his hips and lift the hips slowly and gently upwards. Loosen by shaking gently, lower and repeat four times.
3. Kneel at one side of the child, reach across his body and place one hand on his shoulder and one on his hips, slowly roll the hip towards you. (Movement will be minimal at first.)
   a. Repeat four times, then ask the child to move his own hip; stabilize his shoulder if necessary.
   b. Observe other parts of his body for bursts of tension or for initiation of movement. Should this occur stop the task, relax the moving part, then start the task again.
   c. Repeat the roll with the other hip.
   d. Repeat the roll while the child lies on his stomach.
4. Movement toward a goal. With the child on his back have him reach out to touch an object with his foot or knee. Present the object in such a way that he must lift his hip off the floor to reach the object. Watch for and avoid tension or overflow movement in other parts of the body.

Shoulder Differentiation

1. Movements. Proceed as in "Hip Differentiation," on stomach and back.
2. Movement toward a goal.

a. With the child on his back proceed as in "Hip Differentiation." The child now reaches with his hand and arm.

b. With the child on his stomach have him reach out and up to touch or take an object. Require him to lift the shoulder of the reaching arm off the floor.

Waistline Differentiation

1. Have the child lie on his stomach on the floor, push up until he rests on his elbows. Another person kneels across his legs and holds his hips so that they cannot move. The child then pivots his upper trunk in a semi-circle as far as he can to one side and then to the other by "walking" on his elbows or forearms.

2. Have the child lie on his back on the floor, with another person holding his hips as the child pivots his upper trunk.

    a. He is to slide his hand down along his side until he touches his knee or the knee of person holding his hips. Repeat three or four times.

    b. He is to reach for an object on the floor to the lower right and then to the lower left. Repeat three or four times. The object should be far enough away so that real stretching will take place at the waistline. Make sure that he relaxes the muscles at the waistline on the side to which he turns.

    c. He is to sway back and forth without reaching toward a goal. All items under b. and c. above should be performed on a smooth surface where there is a minimal friction present. The movement should be initiated at the waistline. Do not permit the child to use his head to move himself.

3. The child should lie on his back with his arms out to his sides. Another person stabilizes his shoulders as the child lifts his knees to his chest; feet should be off the floor. He then moves his knees to the far right until they touch the floor, then to the far left. Make sure the child relaxes in each position, before he moves in the opposite direction.

The legs are to move in unison, but not to be *tied* together. If the child finds that holding both legs up is too difficult, he may perform the task by having the knees bent, and feet on the floor. Continue the tasks until the child can perform them without another person stabilizing the non-moving portions of his body.

KINESTHETIC AWARENESS

After the child learns to relax and differentiate the parts of his body, it may be necessary to work for additional kinesthesis to develop control of each part before controlled coordination becomes possible. Many of the movements are the same as those for relaxation but the emphasis is different. The kinesthetic sense provides the most direct information concerning any overt response of the child. Kinesthesis, the sensations from the muscles and joints, *always* occurs whenever movement takes place, and likewise there is no movement without the generation of kinesthetic impulses. Kinesthesis, therefore, provides *direct* feedback whenever movement occurs.

Other senses provide indirect feedback. Visual stimuli can be used for feedback *if* the movement is within the visual field and *if* the vision is unobstructed.

Some children give up or ignore kinesthetic feedback and depend entirely on external clues. They pay little or no attention to the kinesthetic data but try to control the response directly with visual or auditory feedbacks. The results are, on the one hand, frequent disruptions of the response resulting from the intermittent nature of its control, and on the other other hand, undue attention to the control of the response at the expense of its purpose or its integration with other responses. It is important that these children be helped to develop kinesthetic awareness and establish or re-establish kinesthetic feedback.

Others, who are hyperkinetic, receive so much kinesthetic information that it is impossible for them to isolate the specific feedback. Some hyperkinetic children can learn to relax first, then learn to isolate the muscles and joints needed for specific movements while others may need to isolate some specific movements before they can relax.

A third group attends to the specific feedback but is using the wrong set of muscles. Such children may tighten and use the tendons at the back of the knee for all leg movements or use shoulder and elbow movements to control his wrist and hand. They must learn to relax, then learn to use, attend to and control the proper muscle groups.

TEACHING KINESTHETIC AWARENESS

Aims

1. To teach awareness of the muscles and joints to be used for each movement.
2. To teach coordination of the movements of the muscles and joints.

3. To teach the proper use of muscles and joints in purposeful situations.

4. Legs.

    Part 1

    a. Child lies on his stomach on the floor or a mat.
    b. Manipulate the muscles in the thigh of one leg with continuous movement across muscle with flat of hand until loose. Use slight pressure.
    c. Present verbal information along with the manipulation as to the state of the muscle (it is *tight, loose,* etc.). The child is not to make any movement at this time.
    d. Briefly manipulate the calf muscle to be sure it is loose.
    e. While holding the leg at the ankle, slowly raise the lower part of the leg as you massage across the thigh muscle, slowly lower leg, continue massage.
    f. Raise and lower leg slowly without massage. Should overflow be observed in other parts of body, stop the moving part or relax it. Pay special attention to hands and to toes, as the extraneous movement many times occurs in these areas.

    Part 2

    a. The child lifts the lower part of his own leg slowly upward.
       (1) It must not flop towards the buttocks, but lower slowly.
       (2) It must not fall towards the floor, but lower slowly.
    b. Call attention to the muscle the child should use during this movement (the thigh muscles), verbally or by touching.
    c. Be sure calf stays relatively loose.
    d. Repeat four times with each leg (no counting) and when this goes well (no tension) try both legs together.

(If the child has difficulty with control of his legs as they move downward, place your hands at ankles—do not hold, just furnish the control. This should be only temporary.)

    a. Semi-supine position.
    b. Blindfold child if necessary to emphasize kinesthetic feedback.
    c. To teach awareness, manipulate the muscles in the thigh of one leg until loose. Use long, even movements. Present verbal information along with the manipulation. (It is *tight, loose,* etc.) The child is not to make any movements at this time.
    d. Manipulate the muscles in the calf until loose. The leg may be flexed. Support it in this postion by holding at the ankle or at the knee.

e. Move the foot up along floor towards the child's buttocks; with one hand placed under his knee, and another at his ankle, move the leg down. Muscles must stay loose. Place paper under foot for ease of movement if the child is working on hard surface; place foil under foot if working on carpeting. Should you experience tension, work with the child in a supine position.

a. The child flexes his knee as he moves his foot along the floor towards himself. He must keep the muscles in the calf loose and use the thigh muscles.

b. He returns his leg to the floor and relaxes.

c. Repeat the above—no more than four times (each pair of movements equal one movement).

d. Guide the child's leg upward if necessary. Should the knee move out to the side, the child is avoiding use of the muscles that you are trying to educate. Return to supine position if this movement is difficult to obtain without tension in semi-supine position.

a. To be initiated when the above is going well.

b. The child lies in a semi-supine position.

c. He moves his leg out to the side a short distance and then back to its resting place. Repeat five times with each leg.

    (1) Should the movement be difficult for the child, teach the movement in the same manner as above.

    (2) Should movement occur in the opposite leg or in either hand, hold or relax those parts.

    (3) Should the movement be initiated at the foot, relieve tension in foot and/or ankle, hold the foot, touch the upper leg and ask him to move the leg from that point.

    (4) Repeat without the hold.

    (5) Watch for facial tension—remind him to relax mouth or jaw if it occurs.

    (6) Blindfold if more tension occurs with eyes receiving information.

a. Child lies in a semi-supine position.

b. Working with the entire leg, rotate it gently from the hip a small distance from side to side.

c. The knee should be flexed and resting on your hand, the foot off the floor. Make small circles with lower leg, rather than the turn as above.

    (1) As above but with foot resting on the floor.

    (2) Repeat with each leg.

d. Ankle: Teach by manipulating each ankle in circles in each direction.

Part 3: Repeat each part; have the child copy each movement with the opposite limb. For example, any of the above movements will be made with one limb. The child must then transfer the movement to the other limb without being "moved" through it first. These movements may be done blindfolded, with other side, or simultaneously.

Part 4: Ask him to make any the movements above. (Vary their order or presentation.)

Part 5: Repeat all of Parts 1-4 with the child watching himself move.

Part 6: (See section on Movement Control.) Movement against resistance will be applied to all of the preceding tasks in the following manner when the movement asked for seems to be going well (smoothly, controlled, with no overflow into any other part of the body).

a. Initially apply minimal resistance to a movement. Do not begin to resist the movement until the child has begun to move.
b. Movements:
    (1) Flexion and extension of leg (position, supine or semi-supine). Hold the ankle during up or down movement.
    (2) Flexion and extension of leg (prone position).
        (a) The child should push against the hand in either direction. (Hand positioned just above the ankle.)
    (3) Rotations:
        (a) Whole leg—pressure at thigh
        (b) Lower leg—pressure at ankle
        (c) Foot—pressure at foot
    (4) Angel movement:
        (a) Outward and inward movement; use flat of hand at either ankle or thigh.

5. Shoulders

Part 1:

a. The child lies in a supine position upon the floor and should be blindfolded to increase attention to movement.
b. Loosen a shoulder by shaking gently and as you say to the child, "I am moving your shoulder up" move his shoulder up. Hold his arm gently just above the elbow.
c. Repeat the above using the down movement. Do not always start with the up movement.

d. Repeat with other arm. If the child's shoulder comes forward, place a hand or a bean bag on the shoulder to help him become aware of the upward movement.

Part 2:

a. Loosen the shoulder, as above.
b. This time the child must make the movement. The opposite shoulder must not move; should any overflow movement occur in feet, hands, etc., manipulate these parts until loose and try the movement again. Be sure the movement is slow and controlled.
c. The next movements should be against resistance.
d. Let the child begin the movement of the shoulder, then hold back on the arm just above the elbow. Initial, resistance should be minimal. Resistance will help the child become more aware of the movement because of the contraction and relaxation that occurs and also because the child now has to really work on the movement he has learned.
e. The tasks above should be repeated while the child is in the prone position. The movement is easier if the face is turned away from the moving shoulder, as the chin impedes the upward movement.

6. Arms

Part 1:

a. Have the child lie in a semi-supine position.
b. Blindfold him to emphasize kinesthetic feedback.
c. Manipulate muscles in upper and lower arm similarly to instructions for leg.
d. Give verbal information.
e. Flex the arm, support elbow if necessary and move the lower part of the arm towards the child with the hand turned in the direction of the movement.
f. Same as above, but move lower arm out, hand turned in direction of movement. The person working with the movement should keep his hand on the child's hand during these movements.
g. Move the arm as above—in and out, in a continuous movement.
h. Have the child move the opposite arm in the same manner. (You may need to support.)
i. Apply resistance to the hand in both directions so that the child will now use the muscles to which he has been attending.

Part 2: Rotations

a. Support the arm as you slowly rotate it from the shoulder (turn it gently back and forth).

b. Next support the arm at the elbow as you turn the lower arm (held in a flexed position) back and forth.
c. Support the arm at the elbow (in a flexed position) as you move the lower arm in small circles.
d. Rest the arm on the elbow as you move the hand at the wrist back and forth and in a circle.
e. Repeat all of above with the other arm.
f. Again move the child's arm as above; see if he is able to copy the movement with his other arm.
g. Next ask the child to make the movements as you apply slight resistance. (See section on movement control.)

Part 3.

a. The child now watches as you make all of the movements with his body parts.
b. The child watches as he makes the movements, without and with resistance.
c. The child must now put all these movements to work as they must be meaningful in terms of his own environment. He should try scribbling, bouncing balls, swinging a rope, using a screwdriver or pliers, opening and closing jars, cleaning windows.

MOVEMENT CONTROL

In normal development a child differentiates his movements in sequence and integrates each with the next in an orderly way, thus developing organization in development. At this stage the child can go from one movement to another within a pattern and move from one section of his environment to another in a series of steps. As he interacts with his environment and performs tasks requiring more precision he should learn to control and smooth out his movements. He should become aware of them from their initiation to their completion. Movement thus becomes continuous rather than a series of steps. He learns movement control.

Some children, however, fail to develop adequate control of the differentiated parts of their body. Their explorations are sporadic and haphazard due to lack of kinesthetic awareness and /or excessive body tension. Their movements are unpredictable and their deficits fall into three categories. One group includes those children who have difficulty initiating a familiar movement. If required to move suddenly they often refuse or fail. They also have difficulty going from one movement to another. In games they either want to make the rules or they refuse to participate. By making the rules themselves they can adapt the game to their own performance possibilities. In the classroom they spend more time getting into a task than they do performing as they dabble and daydream the day away.

Another group includes the child who has difficulty initiating movement, but once his actions go off they either have no goal or fail to achieve a goal. Such a child may thrash out with his arm in the direction of a stimulus but exert no direction over the movement after it is initiated. The movement may or may not result in contact with the stimulus, depending on the accuracy of the initial direction. If contact is made it leads to termination of the movement only if the stimulus is substantial enough to stop the arm thrust. If not, the movement continues on through the stimulus until it is mechanically stopped by the length of the arm.

Such a child is often accused of pushing, hitting and throwing when he was simply moving without control. He is the child who beats upon the person or animal that he wanted to pet or caress; the child who crushes or strangles the one he had planned to love.

After the child has learned to intitiate a movement toward a stimulus he must learn to stop the movement as soon as contact is made with the stimulus; that is, he learns to control the termination of the movement. Normally the young child spends months learning to reach a stimulus and then takes additional months learning to stop at the appropriate time so that the stimulus can be grasped and manipulated. He then has control at the point of initiation and at the point of termination, but there is very little control during the movement. The initial control sets the direction in which the movement is to go. The termination control determines when it will cease. Between these two points there may be minimal direction or control. If control between initiation and termination is lacking, the child cannot correct the movement even if he sees that it is erroneous, for he has no control of the movement and therefore cannot alter it during its course.

A child with this two point control is frequently seen moving rapidly and explosively. Series of movements are not smooth, but a succession of jerks resulting from reorientation at the beginning and end. He goes dashing through life always on the brink of disaster, yet he usually manages to avoid danger by using his stopping mechanism. In the classroom he talks or reads until he has to stop to catch his breath; he writes rapidly and often unintelligibly. He is exhausting to live with, for he is never still. To remain immobile, he needs to maintain static control over time, but cannot for he does not have this control. With such partial control the child receives no information during the movement, nor can he use information made available to him while he is moving. This is why he moves so rapidly and explosively. He is the master of his response only at its beginning and ending.

Before he can process incoming information and hence learn, he must be able to monitor the movement on the basis of information generated during the movement. To learn movement control, the child must be made aware of the basis of his problem where before he was aware only of the end result. It does no good to say "stop," "sit still," be quiet," "get busy," or "stop pushing," to a child with inadequate movement control. Such reminders call his attention to the end result of his deficit. What he needs is an awareness of his lack of inner control and then help in learning that control.

TEACHING MOVEMENT CONTROL

CONTROL OF INDIVIDUAL BODY PARTS

Initiation

1.   To develop immediate initiation of movement, use a verbal prod to cue the child's movement. (Movement, Level I) Assign a simple task requiring the movement of a limb. Prod the limb with your hand as you give the command to move it up and down, or out and back. As soon as the child moves easily with the combined prods (touch and auditory), discontinue the touch, but continue with the auditory cue.

Simple verbal directions such as: *out, back; up, down; 1, 2, 3* may be used first. Next use sounds. Explain to the child which sound will be used; then demonstrate how he is to move when he hears it. For example: clap your hands each time an arm is to come up or down. The clap-prod triggers the movement in the same manner that the verbal directions did earlier. Other prods can and should be introduced: slap the table, ring a bell or stamp a foot.

After the child learns to initiate, he often moves explosively and with too much force. When this happens he is usually using more than the necessary muscles. Get him relaxed, then help him isolate the needed muscle groups by massaging them before and during the movement.

Termination

To teach a child to stop a movement, it may be necessary to physically stop the moving arm or leg as it reaches full extension or a goal. The teacher must hold that part in place until she feels it relax or release, before the next movement occurs. For example, if the child moves his arm up, stop the movement when the arm is fully extended and hold it there. When the child relaxes or "lets go" tell him to move it down. Stop the arm again and wait for relaxation to occur before telling him to move it up again.

When the child is able to stop the movement and release the tension, begin using auditory cues: "up, stop, relax," then "down, stop and relax." Have the child repeat each movement several times.

When the child is able to stop a movement on command, use other devices that will require the child to listen and to look without another person furnishing the prods. Objects that will topple easily, or make a sound if the movement does not stop on time may be used. The child may also cue himself by saying "up, stop, down, stop" and so on.

Two or more children working together at this stage can make the above task into a game. Line up three of four objects as goals and ask the child to move his hand, foot, elbow, or other body parts towards one of them. He is to stop just as he makes contact with the object so it will not fall over or make a sound. He then moves his hand back to its starting place. The child is to repeat the above procedure with each object. When he finishes give him a score for the number still standing. Each child takes the same number of turns. The one with the highest score will win.

Observe the children carefully when they reach this stage, for some will have developed controlled stopping but not precision stopping. They will stop near the goal and then use atypical means of contact with it. When asked to take and place an object, they do not move the hand, stop and grasp the object all in one smooth operation. Instead they look at the target, then as the hand moves in to make contact with the target, the eye glances away and the child makes contact as best he can. The system is impractical for it relies on estimation rather than actual knowledge of how and when contact will be made. To develop this knowledge, the eyes and hands must be involved in the task simultaneously throughout the entire performance.

Control and the Visual-Motor Match

The inability to use the eyes and hands simultaneously over time may result from motor or visual control difficulties or from inadequate information from sensory avenues. Thus, information that is received may be disorganized or unrelated. The child has not learned to match the information from the eyes and the hands so he shifts back and forth between the two, getting what information he can. If it is necessary to develop adequate reaching and grasping, the eyes must stay on the target until the hand makes contact with it. Controlled taking and placing usually solves the problem regardless of whether the infor-

mation going into the system or integration is at fault. If it is necessary
to help the child develop this control refer to "Ocular Control" in this
section.

The child who has learned to stop but who has not made the visual
motor match can be readily spotted in the classroom as he hesitates
when drawing a line, or prior to a directional change when writing. The
number of stops and the distance in between depend on how well he has
worked through his directional problems and how much he can perform
from kinesthetic memory. He may also experience these additional
problems:

1. He looks, then writes until he loses the pattern, then looks and writes
   again, but never looks as he writes.
2. A straight line may be a series of starts and stops.
3. Hesitations are seen at each change of direction when copying letters
   or words.
4. Hesitations also may be noted at the end of each letter or syllable
   or anywhere within the word as the child overshoots and must re-
   orient visually.

Control of a Movement Between Initiation and Termination

Before the child can learn to control his stopping mechanisms he
must learn some control within the movement itself. The first cues the
normal child uses to develop control of a continuous movement are tactual-kinesthetic because the match is automatic. As a part moves along
a surface, the tactual and kinesthetic information are being received
simultaneously by the brain.

1. Exaggeration: For teaching purposes, learning can be accelerated if
   either tactual or kinesthetic awareness is exaggerated. Thus if the
   child needs to learn control of the movement of an arm, he will receive more information about the movement if he is required to move
   it along a surface which creates strong tactual feedback, and if, at the
   same time, the movement is resisted so that the kinesthetic feedback
   is emphasized. Tactual cues can be exaggerated by having the child
   move a limb:
   a. across a variety of surfaces
   b. by pressing the moving part against the surface

The moving part can be resisted as it moves by:
   a. holding it against the surface as it moves
   b. putting a weight on the moving part
   c. causing the part to push a weighted object

Sometimes it is necessary for movement across a surface to make enough noise that the child can also use auditory cues to maintain control. For the child who cannot, at this point, monitor his movements with his eyes or whose vision interferes, it may be easier to get results if his eyes are covered so that his full attention can be given to the tactual-kinesthetic information. If the eyes are not attending to the moving part, they are attending elsewhere, and conflicting information will be coming into the system.

2. Individual movement coordinated with vision.

As control develops, the extra stimulation used (rough surfaces, sounds, etc.) may become less intense until they are the same as those normally experienced in everyday life. At this point, vision may be introduced to the task. The child should look in the direction of a moving part. Later, he follows it with his eyes as it moves.

3. Movement of combined parts. As soon as the child is able to control the movement of individual parts, ask for a variety of combined movements.

   a. Bilateral movements using both arms or both legs.
   b. Unilateral; one arm and one leg on the same side of the body move at the same time.
   c. Cross lateral movements; the child moves an arm on one side of his body at the same time he moves a leg on the other side.

chapter 3

Behavior Control

Appropriate behavior, like movement control, is learned. Undesirable behavior is also learned. As stated earlier, many undesirable behaviorisms result from lack of movement control. Others are the outgrowth of the child's need to manipulate himself out of situations and tasks with which he cannot cope because of immaturity, lack of movement control and information resulting from his inability to integrate the data that he does possess. If over a period of time a large percentage of the demands made upon him are beyond his immediate capabilities, he becomes adept at using manipulative, resistive or evasive behavior to avoid the frustration of repeated failure. After a while he finds the procedure so effective that he uses it as a means to avoid tasks that he prefers not to perform, as well as the ones he cannot do. Eventually he realizes that there is power in manipulating others and he becomes a miniature dictator.

RE-STRUCTURING BEHAVIOR

The re-structuring of behavior requires observation of the child's behavior, his abilities and disabilities, plus some self-analysis by the adult or adults who wish to change his behavior.

Teachers and parents often encourage or discourage adequate behavior by their reactions to it. Quite often they do not realize that attention encourages undesirable performance. They laugh at the child's antics, continually find fault, punish, talk about him in his presence, do everything for him, show unnecessary concern when he fails, and so on. At other times, the parent or teacher knows that he is influencing inappropriate behavior, but he does not know how to change his approach; the proper approach must be learned.

To change a child's behavior, it is first necessary to know some of the reasons why a child behaves atypically. He may lack movement control or his control may be limited or too gross and rigid. The section on movement control indicated how and why lack of movement control results in atypical behavior. It also interferes with exploration and generalized learning. Such a child has difficulty elaborating and integrating data because his explorations are not systematic. Systematic exploration is dependent upon movement control, including visual control.

When the child finds the gathering and integration of information difficult, he tends to hang on to and repeat that which he has learned and avoid anything new. It simply isn't worth the supreme effort that he must exert to organize himself to perform. His repetition of the old is not perseveration, for in perseveration the child is not aware of a new stimuli; it does not exist. No, this is more a form of rigidity or resistance. The child knows that a new stimulus has been presented. He even has an idea of what is wanted of him, but he must avoid it, because he knows from past experience that his lack of control or his inability to organize will not permit him to make the necessary adaptations or that to do so will require super-human effort on his part. Therefore he ignores, day dreams, says "I can't," removes himself from the task, withdraws, or distracts the teacher from the task with his antics or verbalizations. Because of the rigidity or his inability to move readily from one performance to another, he does not introduce variations into his own play or work, nor can he act on variations presented or suggested by others. Learning becomes more and more limited.

If his environment continues to make demands that are beyond his capabilities and to pressure for performance without correcting the internal interferences, he begins to substitute splinter skills for actual learning. When he cannot substitute and the pressure continues, he learns to manipulate the persons in his environment. He may also agressively resist or use a combination of the two.

Splinter skills are an inadequate way of learning for they cannot be integrated or generalized; they cannot become a part of the overall pattern of learning. Frequent examples of splinter skills can be seen in every classroom. Rigid balance is a splinter skill. Somewhere in the sequence of learning the child could not handle the requirements for balance, so he substituted overall tension to keep himself erect. He had to avoid tasks that required dynamic, flexible movements and many learning experiences were missed while others were learned inadequately. The leaner in the classroom may be leaning because seated balance is not adequate. As a result he may have difficulty holding his paper as he writes or his book as he reads. He may also splinter writing because he must use the wrist of his writing hand to hold the paper and can thus use only tight finger movements to execute the formation of letters and words. Other children are not developmentally ready for writing in kindergarten; but a teacher sticks a pencil in their hands and says "write" and they find a way. The results, however, are most inadequate and writing ability grows worse as the demands increase.

There are also children struggling through reading by occluding one eye, by changing from one eye to the other or by rigidly fixating on one word after another, because they were required to read before they developed visual control of the two eyes. Others may have had to rely on memorization of facts in math because written and oral number combinations were presented before they had a chance to learn that numbers represent groups of objects in space. That is, they were not aware that the number 3 represents (is a symbol for) a group or set of three objects. Thus they do not realize that $2 + 2 = 4$ because the putting together of 2 groups of 2 results in 4. Such children only memorize addition and subtraction facts and the facts are not related to reality. They represent nothing in their environment. They stand alone—integration with other facts is difficult or impossible.

When the child cannot satisfy the demands made upon him by his parents, peers or teachers by substituting or splintering, he learns to manipulate or side-step performance. In relationships with his peers, he may choose to play with children younger or less aggressive than himself. He becomes the leader, sets the rules, call the plays and so on. Another child plays with children older than himself, because they do not expect him to keep up with them, or to accept equal responsibility. A third child withdraws and spends a lifetime on the side lines as a spectator or, worse yet, lives alone in his own private world. When relating to his parents or teachers he may play on their love or pity for him. He may learn their limitations and manipulate them in such a way that he prevents them from giving him a task in which he might fail.

If these substitutions work, splinter skills are accepted and peers and adults permit themselves to be manipulated. Life may not be too hectic but learning is certainly limited. More often than not, it doesn't happen that way. Parents and teachers become concerned because the child does not play with other children. They become concerned because he does not pay attention. The fact that he does his school work one day but not the next or begins to fail in school is bewildering. They have his ears tested, only to find that he hears well. They have his eyes tested, only to find that he can see. Glasses may be prescribed but still learning does not improve. They request an IQ test but the results are within the normal range. Finally they send him to a psychiatrist, who may say he has no emotional hang-ups. The psychiatrist may then counsel the parents and work with the child only to come to the following conclusions: lack of motivation, not accepted by the parents, too pressured and so on. If the "not accepted by parents" theory is given, the parents seek additional counseling, and as one mother said, "we learned to understand and love our child even though he is still manipulating us and not learning but we are having difficulty accepting the fact that nothing can be done to change him." If the "too pressured" diagnosis is accepted, fewer demands are made and the child is passed from room to room failing most of his subjects. Sometimes his frustrations decrease and sometimes they increase.

Should the "lack of motivation" diagnosis be accepted, the pressure is on. After all, if the child has no vision or hearing loss and if his IQ is normal, then he is just lazy. There is no reason why he shouldn't be learning and everyone pressures him in their attempt to motivate him. This procedure seldom works. The child's own underlying deficits have not been taken into consideration and corrected. Soon the child is in real trouble; he is no longer allowed to avoid, side-step, day dream or say "I can't," but neither can he meet the demands. He begins to use more aggressive means of avoidance—he yells, curses, runs away, destroys things, throws tantrums or withdraws deeper and deeper into himself.

When he learns the aggressive resistance works, he becomes unbearable to live with. He plays one adult against another. He is an angel when things go his way, or as one mother put it, "when he is asleep." He is a demon when they don't. The price of peace at home and at school goes higher and higher. Such a child is crying for help; he cannot change his patterns of movement, behavior or learning. Although he has gained complete control of his environment, he is not happy.

It is possible to help such a child, but a new approach is needed. The old method of attacking the end results without finding and correcting the causes has not worked. Parents and teachers have endlessly insisted that the child get busy, be quiet, finish his work, not make a mess, and so on. Since all of the preceding demands require movement control, movement control should be taught whenever a child cannot respond to the normal demands for control. To do so, it will be necessary to push through, to combat the child's rigidity, avoidance or resistive techniques. It will also be necessary to know the child's level of learning, that is, whether he is performing at the motor-perceptual, perceptual or conceptual stage. Otherwise, teachers are apt to present tasks above the child's level of performance and thus encourage further development of splinter skills. Correct analysis is also important. If the child cannot perform a task that is presented: (1) because he cannot make the right movements, or (2) because he cannot elaborate or integrate the data he is receiving, it may be possible to push through and get performance. The result will be another splinter skill, or one pattern of resistance will be broken only to have another develop.

When a child is unable to control his movements and actions, it is the responsibility of his teachers and parents to help him build and structure a pattern of behavior along with movement patterns. To do so, it will be necessary that they be consistent in all their reactions towards the child and that they be constructively consistent. To be consistent is to react in the same way every time a given situation presents itself. The child may then predict how the parent or teacher will react to his behavior. When they are consistent (in a constructive way) the child can attend to the task of learning rather than spend his time and energy figuring out ways to avoid performance. Threats, promises, or coaxing are all non-constructive. They immediately suggest the possibility of manipulation or bargaining and the outcome is therefore unpredictable. Sending the child to the principal may be consistent, but non-constructive, for it serves his purpose if it gets him out of a difficult task. When the adults are unpredictable, the child feels anxious; his predications are constantly unfulfilled. He resists, trying to force them to stand firm somewhere at some point.

As new rules are made and consistently enforced, resistance can be expected as in the past. The new rule will be tested, but once the child is confident that the rule will not be changed or discarded, that those presenting it will react in the same way each time he resists, he will relax, accept it and be happier.

For a rule to be effective, it must be definable and enforceable. It should be so well defined that the child knows instantly when he has broken it; he may argue that you are unreasonable, but he knows that he has not fulfilled the rule. Ignore his arguments and insist on performance.

The simple movements in movement control satisfy these requirements. They are definable and enforceable. Tell the child what he is to move, how he is to move it and how many times. Before starting the movement, explain that, first the rest of the body will lie still and if it does not, you will help him keep it quiet. Second, each movement should terminate in a complete stop. Be prepared to move him and to stop him if he will not or cannot move or stop himself. Change the sequence of activities each session to help the child learn to adapt to change. Since he knows that he is to perform as directed, this will not be an inconsistency. When you have worked through all of his resistive techniques and the child begins to obey rules of movement, the same approach can be used in activities of daily living.

RE-STRUCTURING THE ENVIRONMENT

When a change of behavior is desired in a broader environment, that is, the home or classroom, it is necessary to structure the environment as well as the child. This is done by limiting visual and auditory distractions until the child learns to tolerate them and by establishing and maintaining a structured environment. For the child who is distracted by the sounds in the classroom, auditory information can be structured by limiting the noise and by emphasizing that to which the child should attend. To limit distracting noises, quiet areas can be arranged by using acoustic tile on a folding screen or an isolation booth. Background music often helps mask the normal distracting sounds in a classroom. Putting instructions, science lessons, social studies and so on on tapes for the child to use while studying often helps at home or in the classroom. Earphones can be used to eliminate most of the classroom noises. Visual distractions can be minimized through the use of isolated areas, and by having less clutter in the room and on the walls, particularly in the area of the room faced by the child.

A structured environment pre-supposes a certain number of rules; thus the child learns to tolerate and conform. Sometime in life each person must learn that rules and laws are a necessity and if the rule or law is disregarded there are unpleasant consequences. Most children learn these facts early in life as they come in contact with the laws of nature. For example: If a child loses his balance or stumbles and falls, it hurts; if he climbs up, he must get down or if he touches fire or anything heated by fire, he gets burned. If he runs into a wall, he gets stopped, hurt and/or knocked down. If he plays in dirt, he gets dirty. Some children, however, do not learn from the natural laws for someone is always preventing them from doing so. Climbing is discouraged, or when they do climb, they are taken down; they are not allowed to get dirty or to explore and experiment. They are protected from many learning experiences. Other children are permitted to experience these situations, but because their information gathering processes are blocked, delayed, distorted, or non-consistent, they do not learn. Such children may run into a wall repeatedly but not learn to avoid the wall because of lack of motor control or inadequate perceptual information. These children, too, must learn, but to do so they need special help. They need someone to structure for them, to reinforce repeatedly and consistently until a learning pattern is established.

ESTABLISHING RULES

When establishing rules for any child, but particularly for the child with learning difficulties, the following requirements are necessary:

The rule must be fair.

A fair rule is understandable. The child must be able to understand the terms in which it is expressed. Thus it is necessary to speak slowly and distinctly, and to use simple language. Quite often it may be necessary to demonstrate or move the child through the task, i.e., show him *how* to relax, sit still and so on.

Too often, parents and teachers use terminology the child cannot interpret. He may repeat it or add it to his vocabulary, but still not be able to translate it into action. Such children often use words that are parroted but meaningless.

A fair rule is explicit. Tell the child exactly what he is to do. Do not presume that he knows what you mean. Many terms such as "clean up," "be quiet," "stand on one foot," "sit still" and so on have one meaning to the adult presenting the rules and another to the child. Thus "clean up your desk before you go out to play" may not be enough. What is cleaned up to the child may not be what the teacher had in mind. It would be better to say, "put your books on the shelf, your pencils in your desk and scrap paper in the waste paper basket," and it may be necessary to demonstrate or direct the child in such a performance step by step.

Avoid over-verbalization. Many adults have a tendency to talk too much when working with the learning disabled child. The reasoning seems to be that one must repeat it often if the child is to learn and embellish the presentation verbally to make it interesting. The adults seem to forget that most of the children are battling interferences in the integration mechanism and therefore need more time to process rather than repetition. Even the child who says "huh?" is often asking for time to respond.

The child must be capable of enacting the assigned rule.

He must be developmentally capable; he must possess the necessary differentiated and coordinated movements, perceptual and conceptual, implied in the rule. *Example:* Do not ask the child with poor space organization to copy a whole page of math or the child with inadequate convergence to copy from the board or the non-differentiated child to write with a pencil.

He must have the necessary control to perform and maintain performance. It is unfair to demand that the hyperactive or uncontrolled child sit still, stand in line or write his misspelled words twenty times.

The rule must be enforceable.

The person making the rule must be capable of enforcing it.

1. Physically

   Ask yourself: Do I have the necessary stamina, strength and ability? Will I need eyes in the back of my head or six hands or need to be in too many places at the same time?

2. Psychologically

   Ask yourself: Will my nerves withstand the pressure of constant alertness? Can I remain unemotional as he resists or avoids?

The person making the rule must be willing to take the time to expend the energy necessary for enforcing the rule. That is, he or she must be willing to wait, move and/or act rather than just verbalize. The child quickly analyzes the verbalizer *vs* the enforcer and either ignores or turns off his listening mechanism, letting the adult talk on as he concentrates on his own activities.

Enforcement must be consistent.

Only then can the child predict what the result of his compliance or lack of it will be and feel secure. He will test each rule—that is normal. Testing is his way of assuring himself that the adult will be consistent and will structure when necessary. The child is then free to give his attention to the task.

If the adult is not consistent the child becomes anxious and confused. He must retest each time the adult tries to enforce, for lack of consistency makes it a new rule each time. If inconsistency is prolonged the child tries to structure his life by setting his own rules and he enforces them with a vengeance.

If a rule is not accepted by the child without repeated resistance one of two things may have occurred. The adult has not been consistent or the child is not really capable of performing the task and resists so that the adult will structure the task by putting the child through it physically or directing it step by step.

If it is the first problem, the adult should decide which he wants most —the child to perform or his own freedom from consistency—and he should abide by that decision. If he decides against consistency, he still must be consistent in another way, that is, he must consistently not ask the child to perform the resisted task.

The method of enforcement must be constructive.

To be constructive the child must know at exactly what point he failed or succeeded; therefore the reward or deprivation should be immediate. Reward or deprivation can be social or non-social.

Social rewards are a smile, hug, brief but sincere compliment.

Social deprivations are the stopping of the non-acceptable movement, isolation, withholding of the social rewards. Non-social rewards are food, tokens, gifts, etc. If tasks are presented that the child is really capable of learning, social reinforcement is all that is necessary.

If the relationship between the child and the adult is poor or if skills are taught rather than integrated or generalized learning, the non-social reinforcements are necessary. Non-constructive methods of enforcement are those that suggest to the child the possibility of bargaining. These include threats, promises, coaxing, or anything that is more pleasing to the child than the assigned task. Thus, sending the child to the principal's office is often non-constructive. The child may find it easier and more pleasant to face the principal, who usually gives him a "talking to," than to face the classroom assignment. Most rules can be established within two or three weeks, at which time the child should cease to test the rules each time they are applied. If he does not respond this way, the task, the rule or the application may be at fault.

Occasionally, he will re-test the adult, first to gain assurance that someone else is still in control. If this is the case let him know that you are still calling "the shots." Second, he may have developed to the point where he can handle more freedom; if so, begin giving him more freedom. Move slowly, for at this point he is not ready for complete freedom.

Undesirable behavior may be re-structured once the parent or teacher is aware of its cause and recognizes and accepts the behavior as being poor. Necessary to the change of the unacceptable behavior is a workable technique in terms of what is being changed as well as the stamina and consistency to carry it through.

COORDINATION

BILATERAL MOVEMENTS

When the child can move each limb adequately introduce bilateral activities as outlined in the next stage.

COORDINATION OF UPPER AND LOWER BODY

1. Have the child lie on the floor on his back and touch his toe to his nose or move his foot as close to it as possible. He is to grasp his ankle with both hands to bring it up to his face. Repeat several times with one foot, then the other and finally alternate feet. The child must lift his head and his foot simultaneously.
2. Have the child lie on his stomach, arms and legs extended downwards. Then have him lift his head, shoulders and legs off the floor. His knees should not bend. If the child cannot lift his upper and lower trunk simultaneously, have him practice lifting one then the other. Emphasize the one that gives him the most difficulty. When it becomes adequate, combine the two.

LOCOMOTION

ROLLING

As the child lies on the floor ask him to:

1. Roll over and over and over in each direction
2. Roll to his stomach
3. Roll to his back
4. Roll to his side

Vary the presentation, i.e., stomach to back, back to side, stomach to side and so on. Help the child learn to relax and maintain relaxation in each position and up to a count of twenty. It may be necessary to begin with a count of two or three for the hyperkinetic child.

PIVOTING

Have the child lie on the floor on his stomach, raise up on his elbows and pivot in a complete circle, "walking on his elbows," in one direction, then another.

Have him walk forward using his elbows.

OCULAR CONTROL

PERIPHERAL INFORMATION

It is often necessary to help the child make central vision more functional before he can participate in and learn from visual-motor tasks. To do this he must learn to utilize his fixation reflex and increase his awareness of and dependence upon peripheral data, rather than fusion, as an aid to pointing and aligning his eyes.

Materials Needed:
1. A large sheet of newsprint with heavy dark lines radiating from a central point. The lines provide intense but symmetrical stimulation to the four quadrants of the periphery. The lines should extend approximately fifteen inches out from the center of the chart.
2. Cut a hole in the center of the sheet approximately one-and-one-half inches in diameter. The hole removes most of the foveal stimulation so that the child must rely on peripheral functions in order to perform; it also permits the teacher to observe the movement of the child's eyes.

Procedure:
1. Hang the chart vertically in front of the child.
2. Have the child sit directly in front of the hole at a distance from eye to chart of approximately twenty inches. He must be close enough to the chart so that the stimulating lines will cover at least most of the peripheral visual field. Be sure the child's shoulders and neck are relaxed. His legs should be slightly extended, with his feet flat on the floor.
3. The teacher sits behind the chart with a penlight and in such a way that he can observe the child's eyes.
   a. Sit well back from the hole so that you do not provide foveal stimulation or a target the child can use for cognized fixation.
   b. The chart should be placed so the teacher sits in a semi-darkened area. If there is light behind the teacher the child may follow the shadow of the teacher's arm rather than fixate on the light.
4. Do not tell the child what to do or where to look. No verbalization is necessary other than "sit on the chair," or, if necessary, "stay loose," "let your eyes do what they wish," "let your eyes float."
5. Observe the child's eyes:
   a. When the eyes center on the hole, move the penlight to a position in the periphery of the child's vision. Hold the light close to the paper and quietly turn it on.

      b. The eyes should jump and center on the light.

      c. When the eyes have centered on the light, turn it off.

      d. The eyes should then *drift* back and center on the hole in the chart.

6. This procedure is repeated with the light held at different positions in the four quadrants of the periphery. The light stimulus should be presented at random positions throughout the four quadrants, four to twelve inches from the center.

7. Avoid any systematic order of positions so that the child cannot anticipate where the stimulus will appear.

8 Most children should begin by using both eyes. If this does not work, work with each eye separately. Use an eye patch. Then have the child use both eyes.

9. IT IS IMPORTANT THAT THE EYE(S) DRIFT BACK TO CENTER AND JUMP OUT TO THE LIGHT.

10. Each session should last three to six minutes and there should be two or three sessions a day.

Behavior to Observe:

1. The intense light will cause the fixation reflex to go off. The eyes will jump to the target but should drift to the center as the peripheral stimulation begins to align them.

2. When the light is turned off, an overall peripheral stimulation is left which is slightly asymmetrical. This reflex will bring the eyes back to the center more slowly since the stimulation is only slightly out of balance.

   If the eyes jump back to center, the child is not relying on the reflex but is using central factors to direct the eyes back. He's fixating rather than letting the reflex fixate for him. In this event, it is essential to help the child inhibit this cognitive fixation act. If this can't be inhibited, the technique will only cause him to practice his error. If the child becomes interested in watching the teacher through the hole it may be necessary to delete the hole and stand at one side of the paper to observe the child.

4. If the eyes dart around looking for the next appearance of light, the child is cognizing the task and is attempting to use foveal information to solve the problem. Encourage him not to think about the task but to respond naturally. Variations:

   a. If the child has difficulty bringing one or both eyes into the inner periphery, i.e., to look across his nose, spend more time working in that direction.

   b. The same is true of any other areas that give the child difficulty.

OCULAR-MOTOR MATCH

Body Control

In helping the child learn to reach, it is often necessary to restrain the the chest to encourage and to develop arm movements rather than letting him involve the trunk along with arm movement. Immobilizing the chest will also give the child enough security so that he can concentrate on maintaining visual attention. The restraining may be done in several ways. The child may be seated or he may lie on the floor depending on the amount of balance he has developed.

1. Place a hand on his chest while he is lying in a supine position on the floor. Some children will respond to the pressure of a weight placed on the chest—i.e. a two pound bag of dried beans, etc.
2. The child may lie in a semi-supine position against another person. The person can then stabilize the child by placing an arm over one of his shoulders and rest it diagonally across his body. (The hold should be quite firm.)
3. While seated in a chair the child may be held as above by a person seated behind him in a chair. A more efficient technique may be to wrap a piece of sheeting around his trunk and tie it behind the chair thus leaving both arms completely free. The over-the-shoulder hold somewhat restricts arm movement.

Fixations with Contact

1. Have the child seated, supported and relaxed. Sit facing the child. Use a penlight to utilize the fixation reflex.

   a. Flash the light on then off.
   b. The child is to reach out and touch the light as it flashes.
   c. Continue moving and flashing the light.

2. Using objects. Hold a target in each hand twelve to eighteen inches in front of the child. One target should be directly in front of the child and the other target should be six to twelve inches away, either to the side, below, above, or in front of him.

   a. Vary the targets. Use squeaky toys or objects that shake or rattle. These will provide auditory and visual stimulation.
   b. Vary the method of contact by having the child squeeze, touch or tap the object.
   c. Vary the child's position.
      (1) Have him lie on his back.
      (2) Semi-supine.

(3) Sit with his legs crossed.

(4) Sit supported by another person.

d. Sound one target; then sound the other; have the child make contact with each in turn.

e. Work for a minute or two with each hand, then repeat. Visual motor training that requires the direct services of a second person should be done for three to five minutes, two or three times a day.

f. Move the outer target after each contact so the child can practice vertical, lateral and convergent movements.

g. Permit the child to move his head as he looks from one target to the other until he understands what is required and is comfortable in the task. Then ask him to move only his eyes. If at first he cannot move only his eyes, have another student hold his head for him. As his eyes develop more control require him to control his own head—i.e., keep it still as his eyes move.

3. With grasp and release

a. Using both eyes and one hand the child "grasps and releases" objects that are presented by another person. During these tasks he is required to cross the midline of his body with his eyes and one hand. Use objects that may be grasped and that will require the child's close visual attention. Small hollow plastic hair curlers make ideal objects for reaching and grasping with one hand or foot. The child must place a finger (or his big toe) in the curler, grasp it and then return it by placing it on the instructor's extended finger. The reaching and taking with the foot is excellent for the child who cannot focus at arm's length. It also is an ideal activity for hip and leg differentiation and coordination of leg parts. Most children also enjoy the uniquineness of the task and the challenge it presents.

(1) When asking the child to reach out and touch or grasp an object with his toe, present the target in a variety of positions so that the child must:

(a) Lift his leg to make contact.

(b) Lift his leg with his knee bent.

(c) Lift his leg and extend it out to the side.

(d) Lift, extend and reach across his midline.

(e) Lift with his knees bent and reach across his midline.

(2) When reaching with the hand or the foot, tell the child to take the object. He is to locate it with his eyes and keep his eyes on the object until he takes it. If, however, he locates it with his

eyes and then looks away as he reaches out to grasp, quickly move the object a short distance so that he will miss it unless he watches. If he misses, tell him to try again. Continue to move the object until he grasps it while looking. Next ask him to give it back to you. Hold your hand still and make him place it directly on your finger or in your hand. Do not take the object from him. If he ceases to keep his eyes on your hand while moving the object towards it, move your hand to another position so he will have to look in order to place the object. Arrange the task so that the child is required to cross the middle of his body, sometimes to take the object and sometimes to give it. Begin with short cross-overs and gradually extend to a distance equivalent to the outer edge of the child's shoulder.

b. Using one eye and one hand. For the child who cannot converge or has not learned to use both eyes as a unit because of a lack of muscle control in one or both eyes, it will be necessary to work with each eye separately, emphasizing movement of each eye into areas where it is not presently being used. (Use the right hand with the right eye one time and the left hand with the right eye the next time and so on.) End each training session with the child working binocularly (using both eyes at the same time). As soon as the eyes show signs of control, introduce the next section.

c. Using both hands and both eyes
   (1) Have the child clasp his hands together and use the extended pointer fingers to grasp and release each object. Clasping the hands and pointing the fingers requires differentiation of fingers. If the child cannot perform the task because of this problem, go back to ocular tasks not involving finger differ-entiation, and in addition, work on the finger differentiation problem. In this activity a single object is used, requiring the child to take it on one side and return it on the other, with both hands and both eyes crossing the midline. If the child had difficulty keeping his hands together, begin with the following task.
   (2) Use a large ball or other object that is large enough to re-quire the use of both hands. Hold it in both hands and present it to the child, insisting that he look at the stimuli as he takes the object (on the object place a small, strong visual stimulus approximately one inch in diameter, i.e., a colored circle).

Next have him return the object to you; keep moving your hands or refuse to take it until he looks. At first, present the ball directly in front of his eyes. After he can make repeated eye-hand contacts, present it from any point within a circle, the diameter of which is no wider than the width between the child's shoulders.

The visual motor tasks should be done for five to ten minutes, two or three times a day. They may be adapted to gym groups where children may help each other, to a home program, or to individual work with the school specialist.

EXPLORATION OF FORM

The child's first impressions of form are called "sensory-motor percepts" by Piaget and "perceptions without awareness" by Vereeken. The child exists in a nondifferentiated, panoramic world that has no detail, depth or order. He moves and manipulates himself and objects but does not think about it, does not attend to what he is doing.

In the second stage he becomes aware of the parts of himself and his own movements and of objects in his immediate environment. One need only observe the child to know when this change takes place. There is an "ah ha" attitude as the child isolates one particular element or characteristic from the whole. He becomes interested in that particular characteristic for its own sake. He no longer is just doing. He is observing and studying what he is doing.

The first "ah ha's" occur in self-movement as the child kinesthetically isolates a movement, then studies it visually, goes on to try it in various ways and transfers it to a corresponding part. He repeats and practices until he can move automatically. He then integrates it with other movements and uses it to act upon objects. Until the movement is automatic, the child does not study the object, but the day comes when he no longer needs to study and observe how he moves and his attention will shift. Again, there will be an "ah ha" as he sees an object as something separated from himself. It becomes a specific element in his environment and he will stand back from it, so to speak, and study it. He will be aware of form outside himself and his surroundings will become his major interest.

DEVELOPING EXTERNAL AWARENESS OF SELF
(TACTUAL-KINESTHETIC AND VISUAL)

Exploration of Hands: Encourage the child to look at his hands as he moves his fingers and hands individually and separately. To encourage visual and tactual attention, have him:

1. Squeeze soft clay or mud through his fingers.

   a. Let the clay or mud dry on his hands. This happens quickly and the skin feels "tight" as it dries, encouraging awareness.
   b. Have him rub and roll off as much mud or clay as possible, then wash the rest off. Encourage visual attention to the task.

2. Use finger paints.

   a. Finger paint to which some sand or grout has been added also increases awareness.

3. Place a hand in warm paraffin and let it cool, then have him peel the paraffin off.

Exploration of the Body.

1. Encourage the child to look at and/or feel other parts of his body.

feet	nose	arms
head	ears	legs
mouth	hair	stomach
eyes	face	back

2. To develop initial awareness it may be necessary for the teacher to squeeze or massage the part and to direct the child's eyes toward the part. A strong visual stimuli may also be necessary.

   a. Shine a light on the part.
   b. Paint it with bright colored paint.
   c. Paint with colored paraffin.

3. Have the child rub or massage the part; for example, have him rub up and down his whole leg when teaching awareness of leg.

4. Have the child move the named part.

5. Have him touch the named part.

6. Have him name the part as you touch (child is blindfolded) or point to it.

CONTACT OR PREHENSION OF OBJECTS

1. Opening and closing the hand—Have the child squeeze a sponge, soft not sticky clay, a piece of crumbled paper, and so on.
2. Striking (causality)—Have the child strike objects with his hand, foot, head, both hands to make them move, jiggle, sound and so on. Supply safe objects of materials that encourage petting, rubbing and stroking.
3. Grasping. Supply a variety of objects and opportunities for the child to use a variety of grasps from palmar to pincer.

OBJECTS AS EXTENSION OF SELF

Supply the objects and opportunities for the child to use objects for shaking, waving, pounding or striking.

VISUAL AWARENESS OF OBJECTS

1. Encourage the child to take an object in his hands and observe it from various angles. Use a variety of grossly different objects.
2. Make a game of fixating from one object to another.
3. Have the child observe visually a falling object.

   a. The object falls and lands within the child's visual field.
   b. The object stops beyond the child's visual field. If he searches for it, the object has some permanence.

4. Have the child search for objects that are only partially hidden. Show the child several familiar objects. Then have him leave the room as you partially hide them, that is, a small portion of each object will be visible.

SIGNALS

Encourage the child to attend to signals; have him:

1. Identify what he hears and then look to see if he was right.
2. Say what he thinks a visual stimuli will sound like, then sound it to make sure.
3. Explore an object tactually and then look to see if it looks like it felt. (Naming not necessary at this point.)
4. Examine a new object with his eyes and say how he thinks it will feel. He then can handle it to see if it feels as he thought it would.
5. Gradually uncover familiar objects to determine which signal qualilities the child is using to identify the objects. Remove the cover from various angles, for example, when he is to identify a dog, start uncovering from the head one time, from the tail another and from the feet a third time. This will encourage him to attend to more and more of the elements that make up the whole.

PRE-VISION OF AN ACTIVITY OR RECOGNITION OF
ONE ACTIVITY AS A PRELUDE TO ANOTHER

The teacher performs the first step in preparation for a familiar activity, then asks the child, what do you think we are going to do now, or what comes next?

IMITATION

Have the child do from imitation any or all of motor activities learned thus far.

chapter 4

The Movements and
Sounds of Speech

The child grows increasingly interested in his mouth movements as he matches tactual and kinesthetic stimuli. He repeats the learned movements over and over, and he experiments with new ones and combinations of them. Imitations become possible.

As he learns to feel and listen, and to listen and look simultaneously, he becomes aware that there is a connection between the movements he makes and the resulting sound. One sensory avenue verifies the other. He is more sure about that which he sees because he also hears. Through the sensory-motor match the child is able to make sense of the stimuli he is receiving; without it, his perceptions will be distorted and limited.

Children with learning disabilities often develop only a limited number of movements and sounds, resulting in limited or unintelligible speech. Two reasons for limited mouth movements and sounds are hypertension and over-attention to his own gross motor movements. All children produce fewer sounds during the periods when they are learning a new movement pattern (creeping, sitting, walking, etc.), but as soon as the pattern is learned there is an increase in vocalization. The child with learning disabilities often spends much longer periods of time mastering his movement patterns. Some never master them; therefore, they cannot give full attention to the differentiation of mouth movements, the making of sounds, or the forming of words.

Inadequate movement control often results in body tension, and if the tension is severe enough in the stomach, chest, neck and face areas it becomes a strong deterrent to breathing and to the movement necessary for speech.

MOVEMENTS

In order to successfully achieve the following, the child must be able to relax.

PROJECTION OF THE TONGUE

1. The child should use his tongue, not his hand or sleeve, when retrieving food on his lips.
2. Hold a lollipop, candy cane or popsicle in front of the mouth (close to lips and then gradually move it out) for the tongue tip to touch. Give him an ample taste before beginning and a small piece as reward when exercises are completed.
3. At home, the mother may allow licking the spoon after baking a cake, cooking pudding, etc.
4. Smear upper and/or lower lip with jam to lick or to explore with the tongue.
5. Place cookie bits between lower front teeth and lower lip for the child to recover by using his tongue.

MOVING THE LIPS

1. Imitation of movements.
   a. Imitate a hand puppet, an attractive picture of a child, yourself, or himself in the mirror. Introduce such movements as a smile, sneer, pucker, disdain, or disgust.
   b. Open and close the mouth; the child first imitates; then he does it himself.

2. Movements with sound; teach the child to make lip movements combined with sound.
   a. The raspberry hum (noisily blowing air through closed lips).
   b. Indian War call (as the child says "ah . . . ah . . . ah . . ." the palm of your hand goes out and in against the lips). Soon he will be using his own hand.
   c. Lip smacking.
   d. Kissing, lip puckers with drawing in of air.
   e. Make the sound "mmmmmmmmm" as the child flips or strokes your lips in an up-and-down motion thus changing the sound. Then stroke his lips as he makes the sound.

BREATHING AND SOUND-MAKING
(VISUAL-MOTOR-AUDITORY)

BREATHING PATTERNS

Continue to encourage the various breathing patterns. If stomach relaxation and rhythmic deep breathing continue to be difficult, the following variations may be helpful.

Have the child lie on his back on the floor, arms and legs flexed. The therapist may kneel astride his legs or at his side and proceed as below:

1. Stimulation of muscles: Massage the stomach muscles and those at the side of the waistline to encourage the child to relax them.
2. Encourage the child to breathe using the chest and diaphram, but not the stomach. Rub his chest between his shoulders and tell him to lift that area of his chest and fill it with air as he breathes in slowly and deeply through his mouth; then tell him to exhale slowly and let the chest fall.
3. After the child can let go and relax the stomach muscles encourage him to draw the muscles back and in. This is important, for the child who is over-tense and who is using stomach muscles to control other parts of his body uses a forward thrust of the stomach muscles. If the stimulation causes the child to thrust outward rather than draw the muscles in or relax them, discontinue.

If the approach above is not effective, sit the child cross-legged, tailor fashion, on the floor. Have him place his own fingers across his stomach and each thumb between the lower rib and his hip bone. Kneel behind him so that his back is supported against you. Grasp his shoulders and gently but firmly push his upper trunk forward and down (make sure that his neck is flexed forward) as you encourage him to exhale. As soon as he exhales, pull his shoulders back up and encourage him to breathe in. Repeat several times, keeping the movements smooth and rhythmic. Continue until the child has developed good breathing patterns and can maintain them while speaking.

VISUAL-MOTOR MATCH

Encourage the child to watch your mouth carefully as you make the necessary movements to produce sound. Work before a mirror part of the time so he can see his own mouth making the necessary movements. Work for the following movements (and sounds) in the order given:

1. Prolonged sounds—introduce squeals, yells and prolonged vowel sounds.
2. Encourage variations in pitch.
3. Encourage the child to repeat a sound several times.

   a. Vowel sounds: eh eh eh—oh oh oh, etc.
   b. Syllable sounds: da da da—ga ga ga, etc.

LOCATING SOUNDS

AUDITORY-VISUAL

1. For near work use sound-making objects to encourage visual fixations and pursuits when working close to the child. Sound the noise maker until the child looks. Continue to sound it as you slowly move it about to encourage visual pursuits of the sound-making object. Use a variety of rattles, "crickets," bells, etc.
2. Encourage the visual location of a variety of sound about the room.

   a. Natural sounds: typewriter, radio, rattling paper, running water, chalk writing on chalkboard, child's voice, teacher's voice, bell, clock, pencil sharpener, etc. Have the child locate the direction from which the sound comes and then go touch that which made the sound.
   b. Extraneous sounds: clapping, snoring, whistling, rattles, and whistles.

3. Supply the child with a variety of sound-making objects to explore, one sound *vs* another.

AUDITORY-KINESTHETIC-TACTUAL

Blindfold the child and have him locate, then touch, an object as you sound it at various positions around, above and below him. The sound should be distinct but not too loud, for vibrations may echo in all directions and cause confusion.

COMMUNICATION

A child performing at the Readiness II Level often resorts to infantile means of expressing himself in order to communicate. Attend to any system of communication that the child may use and accept it. Make every effort to understand him until you can lead him toward more adequate verbal forms of communication.

RESPONSE CONTROL

A child operating at the Readiness II Level also resorts to infantile means to avoid any tasks he cannot or would rather not perform. Think of each child at his performance level rather than at his chronological age, and it will be easier to choose adequate learning materials for him. Once a task that the child can perform is presented, insist that he follow it through to completion and perform it exactly in the manner prescribed. The child will often vary or rearrange the task slightly to avoid his learning difficulties. If, however, he is permitted to continue in this manner, very little learning will take place. If he suggests a variation, tell him, "Okay, just as soon as you do it this way, we will try it your way." Do not let the child gain control of the learning activity.

Remember to structure all tasks and give the commands. The child faced with a difficult situation will use many methods to avoid a task at which he thinks he might fail. He may try to make minor changes or resist, act foolish, throw a tantrum, disturb others, giggle, develop aches and pains, and so on. Stop these behaviors; if this is impossible, work right through them (continue with the task as presented, ignoring the resistance).

Many behaviorisms are self-defeating, disruptive to training, and impossible to terminate through outside negative reinforcement. Swatting, reasoning or pressure from other children seem only to increase the behaviors. Thus the behavior itself must become inherently punishing to the child. To accomplish this, the child must be made to "over-do" the behavioral sequence in question.

Thus, the child who hits, kicks, throws a tantrum, or uses other methods of avoiding performance can best be dealt with by making his aberrant behavior more uncomfortable than proper performance. If he kicks, sit him on the floor, hold him in place, and insist that he kick until you and he are exhausted. If he bites, insist that he bite on a piece of hard rubber or other harmless but uncomfortable substance. If he throws a tantrum with kicking, striking and yelling, grasp him firmly and tell him to go ahead and "blow." If he stops, tell him to yell some more but add, "When you are finished yelling, you will perform the task." Thus even the control of overt behavior can be achieved through motor performance. It works because it attacks the problem in two ways. It makes task performance more comfortable than non-performance, and it drains off excess motor energy.

Learn to anticipate the child's abortive and resistive moves before he makes them. Often the child is not aware of the origin of the move, or if he is aware, he does not know how to control it; therefore, all punishment after the fact is useless. The child who jumps out of his chair and leaves the task can be brought back a hundred times; still he wins a hundred times. Become aware of what triggers his dash for freedom; move in and prevent it at its source. A change will occur as the teacher, rather than the child, takes the initiative. Once the child has been made aware of the initial move, he knows that he can learn to control his behavior and often does so rather quickly.

For the child who cannot control himself (remain in place long enough to perform), a seat belt can be used. It stops his initial thrust and acts as a constant reminder. As he develops movement control the belt can be loosened and finally removed.

part 3

Pre-Readiness: Third Level

Moving to Learn

chapter 5

Moving to Learn

The child is now ready to coordinate the four quadrants of his body and develop flexibility and control of his wrists, ankles, fingers and toes. He will use his eyes more extensively as he follows objects that he moves and those moved by outside forces. When persons move out of sight, he anticipates their return or searches for them. He imitates sounds and movements, develops a rudimentary knowledge of the constancy of size and shape and experiments with container and contained. He learns to anticipate what is to come and clearly attempts to influence the immediate future.

Later, he improves his balance and masters walking. The use of container and contained is no longer a matter of experimentation, but a purposeful, understood manipulation. He begins to observe and study the relationships between objects and the pull of gravity. He discovers that he can use objects, including other persons, as a means to an end. The displacement of objects is observed and studied, and objects take on permanence. He experiments in order to "see" more clearly and to find new ways of doing things. He purposefully seeks out new experiences where previously he was content to recapture old experiences and explore those he stumbled into or those presented by others.

In the final stage, he loses some of his dependence on others and learns to control many of his activities from within. He becomes aware of certain basic relationships concerning the objects in his expanding environment, and he utilizes these relationships rather than relying completely on his gropings and experimentations. He is ready to compare and relate in a purposeful manner, to recall the actions of others from past experience and to re-enact these in play and make-believe activities.

Summary: The emphasis during this level of development is still on movement, as the child continues to differentiate, elaborate, coordinate and refine it. If the previously learned movements and development of kinesthetic attention to movement have resulted in movement control, the child is ready for multiple and varied opportunities to use his movements to manipulate objects and give tactual, visual, and auditory attention to the manipulations.

MOVEMENT OUT OF RELAXATION (SEATED)

During this stage, as in others, there will be some children who will need work with relaxation. Because of the demands of the finer perceptual-motor tasks, tension may develop. To insure flexible movements and efficient performance, add the following relaxation activities.

RELAXATION OF SHOULDERS:

1. The child should sit in a chair with his legs slightly extended and his feet resting flat upon the floor. He should sit back in the chair so that the chair back supports him. The lower torso should remain relaxed as he works.

   a. Stand behind the child with your fingers over his shoulders and your thunbs on his shoulder blades. Gently rock the shoulders forward and backward.
      (1) Gently move the shoulders up and down.
      (2) Rotate them to the rear (the most difficult direction).
      (3) Rotate them forward (usually where the child carries them).

   b. The child may now try these movements. Should movements be jerky and tense, repeat the above; emphasize the direction that is the most difficult. The arms should remain relaxed.
   c. The child may perform these tasks seated on a stool, on his desk, or in his desk chair.
   d. When relaxation has developed try various arm movements involving the shoulder (making various sized circular movements with his arms).

e. Any of these tasks may be practiced standing if tension does not occur in the seated position.

RELAXATION OF NECK

1. The child should be seated in a chair as in "Relaxation of shoulders."

   a. Sit or stand behind the child, place your hands on either side of the child's head and slowly and gently move it forward and backward, then from side to side; first with chin and then with ear moving toward the shoulder, and, finally, in a complete circle.
   b. If tenseness develops in the neck muscles (cords stand out at the side or back of the neck), stop the movement and massage the tight area, then continue or work back and forth across the point where the jerk or tightening of muscle is felt until it is minimal; then continue full movement.
   c. When the child's head can be moved without undue tension, remove the support. The child should then move his head in the above ways. Be sure that it does not flop, but moves easily in a controlled manner.

      (1) If he lacks control, support again as he moves.
      (2) If tension develops, stop the head and massage the tense muscles until they relax. (The instructor should try the head movements in order to be aware of the range of movement to be expected.)

These activities can be applied at home or in the classroom. For a more detailed classroom application see Relaxation—Readiness I.

MOVEMENT CONTROL

If the child cannot watch himself move or if the use of vision interferes with movement, blindfold him. In this way he now can give full attention to the "feel" of the movement. In order to control movement the child must be kinesthetically aware. The progression is as follows:

1. Kinesthetic awareness—the child's knowledge or "feel" of the movement.
2. When "feel" has been accomplished, vision may be added. The child

watches as he moves. He does not at this time pursue or follow each movement, but observes globablly.

USE OF POSTURE

The use of exaggerated postures and movements may be necessary to break up the child's habitual but inadequate movements.

1. Place the child in an atypical posture and require him to move body parts. He must maintain his posture as he moves.
    a. Have him stand on a block (4-5 inches in height) wide enough for both feet. Ask him to reach, stretch, bend, grasp and release while maintaining balance.
    b. For variation, have him kneel and do tasks similar to those performed while he stands on the block. Hands and knees position may also be used. Remind him occasionally that the trunk is not to sag, hump or twist as a limb is moved.

MOVEMENT AGAINST RESISTANCE

Stress the need to involve and control all moving parts.

1. Have the children play at being a horse and carriage.
    a. Place a towel around the child's hips as he is on all fours, knees or standing.
    b. Another child may pull back on the "reins" as the first child moves forward.
    c. Vary by having one child resist the forward movement. The child may stand in front and place his hand on the other's shoulders, hips, waist, etc., providing just enough resistance to slow him down and make him work at moving.

MOVEMENT OF THE WHOLE BODY

1. To stress movement of the whole body, use childhood games that require stopping and starting on cue. (a command, clap, whistle, bright light, music, and so on).
2. A series of directions may be given for changing position: *sit, stand, jump, lie down, walk around a chair* and so on.
3. If movement is too rapid or jerky, help the child to develop slow, continuous movements.
    a. When the child loses control and moves rapidly, insist that he

come back and move more slowly. In this way he will learn to move as requested and eventually the slower, controlled movements will become habitual.

b. Games which involve slow motion may be used.

c. Be sure movements are continuous and smooth.

BEHAVIOR CONTROL

Behavior problems often originate or increase in intensity at this stage as the child learns that he can use persons or objects as a means to an end. Learn to recognize resistive behavior and to see whether it is used because the task is too difficult, to avoid the task, or to exert control over the adult or the task. Re-read the section on Behavior Control in Stage II, pages 35-43.

DIFFERENTIATION

HEAD AND NECK

1. Have the child lie on his stomach on the floor. He is to push his

   chest away from the floor with his elbows. Then with his weight on his elbows he is to:

   a. Lift and lower his head. Present objects for him to look at to encourage movement. His shoulders must not shift or turn, nor should the arms collapse. Watch for and eliminate any tension or overflow in other parts of the body.

   b. Look from side to side. Use visual targets for maximum turning and do not permit him to turn his shoulders; only the head should move.

2. Have the child lift his chest off the floor, pushing up until his arms are

   extended . His hands should be flat on the floor and the fingers pointed forward. As he rests his weight on his hand he is to:

   a. Lift and lower his head.

   b. Look from side to side. (Do not let the elbows buckle.)

3. With the child on his hands and knees have him move his head as in 1 and 2. Again see that no part of his body moves—other than his head.

4. The child should lie on his stomach on a table, with a pad under his chest and his head over the edge (unsupported). He then lifts and lowers his head.

5. The child should lie on a table on his back with his head over the edge and a pad under his shoulders; have him raise and lower his head.

    a. Perform each of these activities four or five times during each training session until they are no longer difficult for the child.

HIP AND SHOULDER DIFFERENTIATION

Hip Roll

1. The child lies on the floor on his right side with a pad under his head. The top leg is flexed and the bottom leg extended or flexed. His head rests on one arm. The other rests on the floor in front of him. Kneel behind him at his waist, and place one hand on his shoulder. Slowly move his hip backwards and downward; then move it forwards towards the floor. During this movement, the hand on the shoulder exerts counter pressure. Tell the child that he must be as loose as possible and let himself be moved. Call his attention to the movement by saying, "You are now loose and your hip is moving forward," etc. Tell him to think about how it feels as he is being moved.

2. Hold the shoulder and the lower leg, then tell the child to move his upper hip forward and then backward. Do not let him push with his knee; the action should be in the hip. When he is aware of the required movement go on to "3."

3. Again, place one hand on his shoulder and one on his hip. Slowly move his hip backward (or forward), but this time as his hip is back as far as it will go, make a short, quick movement in the same direction and say "pull" (or push). Resist the movement sufficiently to require him to make a counter movement: a smooth, strong, steady pull.

4. After steps 1, 2 and 3 are well established, begin again as in 3 above, except that after the hip has moved back or forward about three-quarters of the way, say, "hold" and increase pressure briefly. At this time an equilibrium has been reached. Now say "let go" or "relax" and be sure that he does relax. If he does not, shake the hip gently back and forth until he is relaxed.

5. Repeat the task five times. Next ask the child to make the movement himself. Following this task, move his hip backward (or forward) without the resistance and ask him to move his hip in the opposite direction. Give the command "hold," then "relax." At first ask for only one such performance, then gradually increase to as many as he can do and still maintain relaxation. Five times should be maximum.

6. When the child can perform both the forward and the backward

movements adequately, ask for alternating movements. That is, after he moves forward, holds and relaxes, have him immediately initiate the backward movement and repeat several times. Finally, have him move the hip forward and backward slowly and rhythmically without the "hold." Repeat each of the steps above with the left hip.

Shoulder Roll

Repeat each of the steps above substituting the shoulder for the hip. When asking for shoulder movements, hold the child's hip and move the shoulder. If the head turns as the shoulder moves have another person hold the head until the child can perform, with his head still and the neck relaxed. (For some children, a bean bag resting on the cheek will provide a sufficient reminder to keep the head still).

Shoulder Thrust

1. Upward Shoulder Thrust: The child lies on the floor on his back, legs extended and arms at the sides. Kneel straddling his legs. Place a hand on his left arm to stabilize it.

    a. Grasp his right arm above the wrist and pull the arm slowly toward his feet. When it reaches full extension give a short, quick stretch toward his feet; at the same moment say "pull." He is to pull the arm upward along the floor moving the arm from the shoulder not the elbow. If the child responds with elbow movement, grasp his arm above the elbow. Resist the movement sufficiently to require him to respond with smooth strong pull. When the right hand is an inch or so beyond the left one say "hold" and increase the resistance briefly. As in the work with the hips maintain a status quo. Then say "let go" or "relax" and make sure that he does. If he does not, shake his arm gently. Repeat three to five times.

    b. Gently and evenly pull the child's arm down; then ask him to move it up, "hold" and "relax." If he bends his elbow, grasp his arm above the elbow. Do not resist the upward movement. At first, ask for only one such movement then increase to as many as he can do and still keep his body relaxed. Five times should be maximum.

    c. Have the child make the movement without any external cues.

2. Downward Shoulder Thrust: Follow the same procedure listed above.

    a. Grasp his right arm above the wrist or elbow and move it upward. When the shoulder is up as far as it will go, give a short, quick push upward; at the same time say "push." Then he is to move the arm downward (be sure that he is moving at the shoulder, not the elbow). Resist the movement to encourage him to make a strong, steady pull. When the right hand is an inch or so beyond the left one, have him "hold" and then "relax." Repeat three to five times.

b. The child should make the movement without resistance or external clues. *Repeat the above procedures with the left arm.* When the child performs both the upward pull and the downward thrust adequately, ask for alternating movements.

(1) Up, hold, relax, then immediately down, hold and relax.
(2) Have him thrust up and down without the hold and relax.
The movements should be rhythmic.

Hip Thrust

1. Upward Hip Thrust: The child is to lie on the floor on his back, his arms at his sides and his legs extended. Hold his left leg to stabilize it.

a. Grasp his right leg at the ankle and gently pull the leg downward. When it reaches full extension, give the leg a short, quick stretch; at the same moment say "pull." Then let him pull the leg upward (making sure that it is moving upward at the hip, not bending the knee). Resist the movement sufficiently to require a smooth, strong pull from him. When the right foot is an inch or so beyond the left one, have him "hold" and "relax." Repeat three to five times.

b. Have the child make the movement without help.
c. Repeat these procedures with the left leg.
d. When the child performs both the upward and the downward thrust adequately, ask him for alternating movements.

2. Move the leg up, hold it there momentarily, relax, then move it down, hold and relax.

3. Have him move his leg up and down without the hold and relax. The movement should be rhythmic.

ELBOWS

Watch to see that the elbows are relaxed and a coordinated part of the whole arm movements. The tense child often carries the lower arm up toward his chest with the elbow locked. If so, it will be necessary to get the elbow relaxed and moving without tension.

1. Put a splint on the child's arm/arms as he walks to inhibit the drawing up process.
2. Continue to use the suggestions for "Movement and Relaxation" of arms in Stage II. Have the child perform in a number of different positions.
3. Require the child to perform a variety of reach, grasp and place activities. Require him to move his arm back and forth, in and out, and in circular movements as the elbow is supported.
   a. Massage across the inside of the elbow.
   b. If tension occurs during self-movement, move the forearm for him.
4. Ask for a variety of movements that require full extension of the arms.

KNEES

1. Observations of knee movements.
   a. The cords at the back of the knees may be too tense.
   b. The child may lock his knees backward when standing because of inadequate muscle balance and control in the leg.
   c. The knees turn in or out. This is usually due to a lack of differentiation and control in the upper leg combined with and possibly caused by a lack of adequate balance.
2. Alleviation of the problems above may be accomplished by the following methods.
   a. Have the child lie on the floor on his stomach.
   b. Grasp the child's leg at the ankle and slowly raise and then lower his leg, flexing the knee as you do so.
   c. When you see the cords at the back of the knee "jump," stop the movement and massage firmly across that area with the flat of hand. When the cords relax continue movement of the leg. Repeat the above technique every time tension occurs at the back of the leg.
   d. When the child appears to be able to let his lower leg be moved up and then down without the "jumping" appearance of the cords, have him repeat the directions above by himself. Movement should be continuous; no jerky movements should occur. Have him move each leg separately.

3. Should these procedures not work, it may be necessary to try another approach to the alleviation of the tightness at the back of the legs.

   a. The child lies on his stomach.
   b. The teacher kneels at the child's feet, grasps both ankles with her hands and with quick (sculling) movements of her wrists moves the legs up and then down. Repeat four times, then see if you can move the leg as described above.

WRIST

Help the child learn to move his wrist. Use a seated position. You may use a chair or a semi-supine position against a pile of pillows.

1. Support the child's arm by holding the forearm; move his hand back and forth, in a hinge-type movement. Stress relaxation—you are to do the movement.

   a. Tell the child to move his hand as above. The fingers do not tighten. The arm stays relaxed, but with tonus.

2. Other movements—same procedure as above.

   a. Side to side
   b. Rotations

3. All of above against slight resistance of teacher's hand.
4. All of above while holding onto object. Be sure only the wrist moves. (There will be slight normal movement of the fingers during some of these tasks.)
5. Shake an object using the wrist.
6. Work with each wrist. Then try both together (VI Coordination - Bilateral).
7. Meaningful tasks using the wrists.

   a. Screwing and unscrewing lids
   b. Turning large knobs
   c. Rolling papers
   d. Wringing wet clothes and so on.

ANKLES

The child should sit comfortably, his feet flat on the floor. Have him keep his heels in one place as he:

1. Turns his feet out and back, separately and together.
2. Lifts his feet up and down, separately and together.
3. Makes rotary movements with his foot.

The movement should be in the ankle and the toes and should be relaxed. The child may perform the preceding motions against resistance. Resist with your hand or tie a light weight to the top of his foot.

FINGERS

Some children have so little tactual-kinesthetic awareness in their hands that it becomes necessary to use tactual stimulation to develop awareness before adequate movement can be learned. Lack of tactual-kinesthetic awareness may appear as lack of tonus or hypertension in the hand and fingers. If there is a lack of tonus, proceed as outlined below. If there is excessive tension, use both relaxation and the following suggestions.

Either of the problems above make writing a laborious process. The child may be unable to hold or control the pencil. Too tight a hold on the pencil must involve other portions of the body, causing overflow movements. The whole upper body and face may be pulled down toward the paper. Because of the lack of differentiation, coordination, and control of the extremities, the child must involve other parts of his body to get enough control to perform, but the control is atypical and exhausting.

If the child is unable to attend to his own hand visually as it is massaged, it will be necessary to begin the hand massage with the child blindfolded to be sure that he attends to the feel of the massage. After a period of time with the blindfold try removing it. Demand that he watch the massage. Any time you see lack of tonus or tension recur, reintroduce relaxation and massage until the child can perform adequately.

Massage (Passive Stimulation)

Specific tactual stimulation of the inner surface of the hand.

1. Begin stimulation by massaging the surface between the child's fingers moving up and down the finger. Use your fingers or a piece of terry cloth, a wash cloth, etc. to do this. For the child with too much tonus, i.e., rigid, tense fingers, begin with relaxation.
2. Next, massage across the base of the fingers and at the base of the thumb. Use the side of your hand in long continuous strokes.
3. Then massage at the wrist with the side of your hand.

Active Use of the Hands

After the massaging, put the hands to work. Stabilize the child's forearm as he:

1. Performs against a variety of surfaces, i.e., rough carpet, soft clay, finger paints.
   a. Have him move his hand from side to side.
   b. Draw his fingers up along the surface to make a relaxed fist, then return to flat position.
   c. Spread fingers apart, then bring them back together.

2. Performance in open space. The child should perform the following:
   a. Wiggle his fingers
   b. Open and close his fingers.
   c. Rub thumb across the four fingers and back.
   d. Touch each finger tip with tip of thumb—Begin with pointer and move to little finger, then back.
   e. Grasp a ball, then lift one finger at a time, then lower them one at a time.
   f. Close fist and release one finger at a time; then lower one at a time.
   g. Finger plays.

3. Gross motor activities to coordinate the hand and arm.
   a. Creeping on elbows, forearm extended in front and hand flat on the floor.

   b. Creeping on hands and knees, hands flat on the floor and pointed forward.
   c. Wheelbarrow walking.

Eye-Hand Activities: Refer to Exploration Form in "Time and Space" on pages 86-91 and to the many suggestions under "Readiness" on pages 104-56.

Introduce Scribbling.   Preparation for Writing, Readiness, Stage I, pages 141-47.

TOES

1. Make sure the toes do not tense as the child performs other tasks and that they can be moved while the rest of the body remains relaxed, (see "Relaxation of Leg," pages 16 and 17).

COORDINATION

BILATERAL

After the child has sorted out and can move individual body parts, introduce bilateral movements (both arms, legs, hands, etc.). When working with bilateral movements the child must learn to initiate and terminate the movement simultaneously. If this is not done and one arm or leg proceeds the other, bilateral movement does not occur, nor does synchrony or "nowness" in time.

COORDINATION OF UPPER AND LOWER TRUNK

1. The child should lie on the floor on his stomach, with his legs straight. Place his arms in one of the following positions.

    He is then to lift his chest and legs off the floor and hold as he rocks forward and back 4 or 5 times. Stop, rest, then return to the starting position. This activitiy may be repeated two or three times.
2. The child should lie on the floor on his back.
    a. Have him lift one leg and his head simultaneously, grasp his foot with his hands and touch his toes to his ear (instead of his nose). It may be necessary to show him how to turn his knee outward from his body so that it does not interfere. He is to touch his ear 4 or 5 times with each foot. He is to lower his head and leg each time, relax, then do it again. (It may not be possible for him to make contact with his ear, but he should move his head and foot as close as possible.)

BALANCE

Many youngsters do not learn static balance during the initial stages of development. If you disturb their orientation to gravity, they will easily fall over. They do not react flexibly to changes in orientation, such as shifts of body mass that occur when a child creeps over a pillow or walks across rough terrain. These children may be helped through the presentation of activities involving changes in orientation.

MAINTENANCE OF STATIC BALANCE AGAINST PRESSURE

The purpose of this activity is to teach the child to hold body position against an outside pressure which changes its direction slowly, smoothly and rhythmically; and to accent his awareness of his center of gravity and the distribution of his weight mass around that center.

There are two stages in learning to maintain balance against pressure. First, the child must realize that he is losing his balance and push back against the pressure instead of falling. Second, he must learn to hold his position against the pressure. If, as pressure is applied, the child lets go and permits himself to be moved or he falls, encourage him to push back. If he cannot, two other approaches can be used. First have him push against a person who can push back in order that he may feel in another what is required of him or make the task meaningful by placing the child on a raised platform. Falling over will become uncomfortable. (Some children will not make the necessary effort unless they feel it is wise not to lose balance.) If he does not resist the pressure when he is in danger of falling, he is not ready for the acitivity and more work should be done to develop coordination.

As soon as the child learns to push back, begin encouraging him to hold his position. Tell the child he is to hold still and not let himself be moved. Let him push someone who can maintain the position so that the child knows what is expected of him.

If he still continues to push back, suddenly release the pressure. He may then fall. Explain to him what he was doing wrong and then try again. When he does manage to "hold" against minimal pressure, tell him immediately that he is doing it right, thus emphasizing the difference between the pushing and holding.

1. On hands and knees. The child should be on his hands and knees with his hands directly under his shoulders, the fingers pointed forward. His knees should be directly under his hips with his entire foot (insteps and toes) resting on the floor. At first his head should be up and his eyes looking at a target at his eye level. When balance is secure he should perform with his eyes closed or wearing a blindfold.

   a. Holding, fore and aft:

   Kneel behind the child and place both hands on the child's shoulders (one on each shoulder). Pull his back towards you. Tell the child to tighten up and hold. Say, "Don't let me push you over."

Gradually increase your pressure and hold for three or four seconds. Slowly release the pressure and move your hands along the back until they are on his buttocks. Push forward for three seconds and again ask the child to hold. Repeat three or four times.

b. Diagonal holding, fore and aft:
   (1) Place a hand behind one buttock and push forward diagonally for about three seconds; then place the other hand on the opposite shoulder and push backward diagonally. As you increase pressure on the shoulder, release the pressure on the buttocks. Repeat three or four times. In other words, you are alternating rhythmically your hands and the push on his shoulder and buttock. The child is to maintain his position at all times.
   (2) Change to opposite buttock and shoulder and repeat as above.

c. Holding, side to side:
   (1) Kneel at the child's side, facing him. Reach across the child and place one hand on his hip and one on his shoulder and pull. Hold for 3 or 4 seconds and release.
   (2) Apply pressure to the opposite hip and shoulder, push, hold and release.

d. Diagonal holding, side to side:
   (1) Kneel at the child's side and place a hand against the child's chest just behind and under his armpit. Reach across his body with your other hand and place it against the lower side of his hip.
   (2) Push his chest away from you and pull his hips toward you. Hold for three seconds, release smoothly, then change your hands to the opposite hip and shoulder. Apply pressure, hold, release. Repeat 3 or 4 times.

2. Seated:
   a. Have the child seated cross-legged on the floor with his hands on knees. Kneel behind him.
   b. Place a hand on his right shoulder, push to the left, hold for three seconds, slowly release as you place a hand on his opposite shoulder, and push to the right. Hold for three seconds; release. Repeat three or four times.
   c. Place a hand on each of his shoulders; push forward. Hold three seconds. Release, then pull backward, hold, release. Repeat three or four times.
   d. Put one hand on each of his shoulders, push forward on one shoul-

der, and pull backward on the other. Hold three seconds. Slowly release. Then push in the opposite direction, hold, release. Repeat three or four times.

FLEXIBILITY

Once the child becomes aware of his center of gravity he must learn to move flexibly around it.

1. On hands and knees:

    a. Rocking fore and aft. The child should be on his hands and knees, his hands placed flat on the floor, a little farther apart than the

    width of his shoulders and slightly forward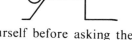

    (Practice the position and movement yourself before asking the child to do it). His knees should be directly under his hips, feet extended and relaxed.

    Ask the child to move his torso backward until his buttocks rest on his heels. His hands should not move or change position in any way. Then have him move his torso far forward until all the

    weight of the trunk rests on his arms.  Once
    he knows what he is to do, have him rock back and forth five or six times, stopping momentarily to relax in each position. His knees and hands must remain as they were originally, at all times.

    b. Rocking, side to side:

    The child should be on his hands and knees with his hands directly under his shoulders and his knees directly under his hips. Now have him rock his whole trunk from side to side, bearing his weight on his right arm and leg then on the left arm and leg. His hands and knees should not leave the floor at any time. Repeat three to five times.

    c. Rocking board:

    Rocking apparatus is available commercially or can be made.

    (1) Have the child get on the board on his hands and knees. His hands should be directly under his shoulders and flat on the board with the tips of his fingers at the board's edge. His knees should be directly under his hips. His eyes should be fixed on

a target in front of him. Do not permit the child to sit down

on his legs. He should look like this: not

this: or this:

(2) Tilt the board forward and then back. The child should shift his body weight smoothly with the board's movement to maintain balance. He should not move his hands or knees. His elbows should not buckle, nor his feet tighten. When he can adjust readily to slow, rhythmic fore and aft movements, move the board in irregular patterns, such as two forward and one back, three back and two forward and so on.

(3) Have the child change his position on the board so that he now rocks from side to side (his body perpendicular to the rockers). Kneel behind him and move him.

2. Seated:

   a. Have the child sit cross-legged (Indian fashion) on the floor with his hands on his knees and his back straight. If he cannot keep his back straight, kneel behind him and push his back straight or walk your fingers up his spine as you tell him to sit tall. You may tell him to reach for the ceiling with the top of his head, or have him practice slumping, then straightening, his body.

   b. Have him practice sitting straight, beginning with a few seconds and extending to one minute. When he can sit erect without undue tension begin the balancing activities.

   c. Encourage him to relax and let himself be moved. If he suddenly jerks or tightens a muscle during the movement, massage the tense area or move him back and forth across that point at which he tenses until the jerk or tightening is minimal; then return to the task.

   d. Support him as he moves.

   e. Finally the child moves himself.

   f. Kneel behind him and grasp his shoulders firmly between your hands and move him in the various patterns listed below:

      (1) Move the child's upper trunk from side to side bending at the waist. The head should lead the movement; the hips should remain stable.

      (2) Push the child's shoulders from side to side as he keeps his head erect and his eyes on a target placed at eye level, three or six feet in front of him.

(3) Tilt the child fore and aft. His head should come forward first.

(4) Push him fore and aft as he keeps his head erect and his eyes on a target.

(5) Have the child extend his arms out to the side and move them with his upper torso and shoulders as he twists from side to side. He is to remain firmly seated while doing so. He may turn his head with the movements one time and keep it on a target another time.

(6) Require the child to reach out in all directions while maintaining balance. Encourage bending, stretching, turning and twisting at the waistline. Have him reach with both hands simultaneously and each hand separately to touch or to take an object. (When reaching with one hand the child *must not* support himself by placing the opposite hand on the floor.)

(7) Place a pole so that it rests behind his neck and across his shoulders. He is to hold it by hooking his arms over it. The hands may or may not hang free. Present targets so that he will have to twist and turn to touch them with one end of the pole, then the other. The targets may be in the air or on the floor.

(8) All these movements are to be relaxed, smooth and rhythmic. Repeat each of the activities five or six times during each training session until the child is doing them well. Next have him perform with his legs extended (more difficult and not possible for those with tight hamstrings). Repeat 1 through 6 on pages 78 and 79.

LOCOMOTION

A great many children with learning disabilities show deficiencies in locomotion. Their movements do not flow freely nor are the children sufficiently well coordinated to explore space. This child needs to develop variations of movements which will permit him to perform in as many different ways as the circumstances of the environment demand.

Crawling gives excellent practice in the differentiation and coordination of the whole body. The movement across a surface adds tactual clues and allows the child to concentrate fully on coordination, since he does not have to be concerned about balance.

MARINE CRAWL

1. The child is to propel himself forward using arms and legs, but is to

keep his stomach flat on the floor and his chest and head low. Within a short period of time he should be able to work out unilateral

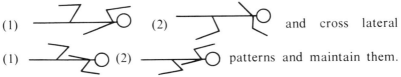

(1) — — — — — (2) — — — — — and cross lateral

(1) — — — — — (2) — — — — — patterns and maintain them.

If he does not, assisted creeping should be introduced to help him
establish the patterned movements.

2. The child who cannot crawl in this manner usually has parts of his
   body that are not working adequately. It may be the upper or lower body, the right or left side or a quadrant. Observe the child as he
   moves across the floor and pinpoint the areas he is not using, then
   help him develop the necessary differentiated movement and coordinate it with the other limbs.

3. The following activiy is recommended for the child who is moving
   and pushing adequately with his leg, but whose corresponding arm is
   inactive or lacks the tonus and awareness necessary to pull forward.

   a. Grasp the desired hand, pull it forward to a point just beyond
      the child's head. Hold the palm firmly on the floor so that the
      child can pull up to it as he pushes with his leg and say "pull."
   b. Tap the desired hand and tell him to move it forward. When the
      child reaches forward, stabilize the hand as he pulls his body for-
      ward.
   c. Tap the hand to identify it as the one to be used.

4. The following activity is recommended for the child who can reach
   and pull with his arm, but whose corresponding leg is inactive or lacks
   the necessary force to push.

   a. Move, or stimulate the movement of, the leg by prodding it into
      the proper position, then hold the lower leg against the floor and
      tell the child to push.
   b. Grasp the foot and knee and place the leg in position and hold it
      as he pushes.
   c. Tap the leg that is to move, then hold the foot firmly against the
      floor.

The goal of this task is to help the child achieve smooth, coordinated
movement. Therefore, give him only the assistance he needs to perform successfully. Encourage his active response to your commands
and gradually reduce your assistance until he is performing on his own.

The marine crawl may be presented by having the child make one
round trip over a twenty-foot course of the distance which can be
covered in three minutes, whichever is less. For the younger child, a fa-

vorite toy can be placed about ten feet away to encourage his movement. When he reaches the toy, let him play with it awhile, then move
it ahead again. Continue only until he can move adequately in each pattern (unilateral and cross lateral) without thinking about how he is going
to move. Then make the task meaningful by introducing an obstacle
course so that he is required to use his crawling to solve movement
problems (over, under, through, etc.).

CREEPING

Creeping is a significant locomotion pattern because of the demand
for cross lateral movements, and cross lateral coordination is significant because of its importance to learning. Usually because they lack
cross lateral coordination, children with learning disabilities often have
difficulty mastering the creeping pattern.

In education, creeping serves two purposes: First, it is a useful
movement pattern, particularly in exploring spaces which are too low or
too confined to be explored in the upright position. Second, it requires
cross lateral coordination. Therefore, it is not desirable to teach creeping by itself. Rather it should be taught along with other activities requiring cross lateral coordination so that the generalization develops
rather than the learning of a specific skill. Furthermore, the correct
creeping pattern should not be taught exclusively. Give the child practice with other patterns (one side against the other, top *vs* bottom, and
the like) so that the contrast between these various patterns can help to
emphasize for the child the nature and function of the cross lateral pattern. Such contrast also contributes to the development of generalization as opposed to specific skills.

1. A child may tend to use one side in opposition to the other. As a
   result the leg and knee on the same side advance together. To correct the pattern:
   a. Place a two-by-two along the floor.
   b. Ask the child to straddle this on his hands and knees.
   c. Place tiles, tape, etc, to indicate where the hands are to go. The
      board separates the action of one side from that of the other and
      prevents any cross over. The tiles tell the child the next movement.
   d. Stand behind the child and hold the leg on the side of the moving
      arm. This insures that the correct knee will move forward. Stop
      after each movement to see that the child appreciates the position
      of his body and how it got there.
   e. If the leg you are holding tends to move, call the child's attention

to this movement verbally. Wait until the movement has stopped then ask him to move correctly. Be sure you give him time to recognize and appreciate the correct movement before you continue.

2. Another child may use the top of his body in opposition to the bottom. Such a child will move both hands forward together, then pull both knees up to his hands.

   a. Use the same equipment as before.
   b. Hold one hand and the opposite leg until the desired position has been achieved by the child. Be sure he recognizes this position before proceeding.
   c. Hold the other arm and leg and ask the child to creep one step. Again be sure he recognizes the new position before proceeding.
   d. Encourage him to stop the movement in the non-active limbs so that you do not have to hold them back.
   e. When the child can perform, decrease your assistance gradually.

3. Variations

   a. Vary the surface: sand, rug, trampoline, a slick surface, etc.
   b. Resist the movement: Resistive creeping is a good variation of the task, particularly if the child is doing all the work with just his legs or just his arms while simply moving the other appendages to give himself support. Ask the child to creep in water, to offer resistance to movement.
   c. Vary the speed.

CLIMBING

Climbing is another activity requiring coordination of upper and lower body, and finally, cross-lateral coordination.

1. Have the child creep upstairs.
2. Have him creep downstairs, backwards
3. Supply a variety of obstacles to be climbed upon: chairs, boxes, blocks, inclined planks and so on. Encourage the use of hands and knees as well as hands and feet.
4. Ladders. Arrange ladders in the following ways:

   (a) Flat:

   (b) Simple incline:

(c) Steep incline:

Have the child move across or up the ladder using his hands and knees, and hands and feet. At first, he may place one hand on a rung, then the other hand on the same rung; then he will move the feet up one at a time. When the child can move without fear or tension in this pattern, help him learn to move across or up the ladder using a cross lateral pattern.

WALKING

1. Sideways

   a. Have the child walk along a narrow beam (two to four inches wide) while holding onto a rope at eye level. He is to walk leading with one foot then the other. If he has more difficulty leading with one, have him practice more often moving in the difficult direction.

2. Walking from hand hold to hand hold.

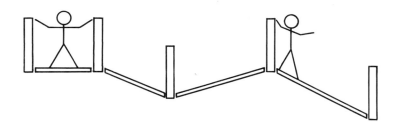

a. Place short, narrow beams between pieces of furniture or other objects that will supply hand holds. Some should be close enough that the child can reach from one to the other. Others should be far enough away to require the child to make a step or two before he can again support himself with his hands.

3. Walking in open space.

Nearly all children with perceptual handicaps are walking in open space by the time they enter school—many of them inadequately, but walking. Even after working through the locomotion patterns above, it may be necessary to perfect the walking pattern. Suggestions for development of a more adequate walking pattern are presented in the next stage, "Readiness."

OCULAR CONTROL AND VISUAL MOTOR MATCH

PERIPHERAL VISION (STRUCTURING THE PERIPHERY)

Many children, in the absence of a structured background, find pursuits and convergence difficult. Conversely, the addition of a structured background may improve ocular control, as it aids in structuring peripheral vision as well as deleting the visual stimuli in the environment which distract many learning disability children.

1. Draw papallel lines on an entire piece of stiff paper or cardboard. Usually an 8½ x 11 sheet of paper will suffice, but paper as large as 18 inches square may be needed.
   a. These patterns should be drawn by hand with a black felt tipped pen to intensify the background structure. Minor irregularities caused by free hand drawing are more desirable than a perfectly symmetrical pattern.
   b. The most intense grid is drawn with double lines resulting in 1½ inch squares.

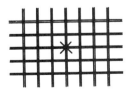

   c. Draw a small red circle or star about one-half to three-quarters

   inch in diameter in the center.
   d. Move the sheet in all pursuit directions including convergence.

(1) The child should point to and touch the target dot as it moves. He should use one hand, then the other, and then both. When using both, the hands should be folded, the pointing fingers extended together. The hand should always remain involved, but the choice of which hand or hands should be random. The child's neck and shoulders must be relaxed.

(2) The target should be held so that the child's arm is slightly bent as he pursues the target with his hand and eyes.

2. As ocular pursuits and convergence begin to improve, limit the background pattern. Do so by reducing the number of lines in the background, use single lines and allow more space on the sheet. Gradually work toward the removal of all background lines.

The child should do the activities for structuring the periphery at least three times a day and for two or three minutes each time until control is developed. Many of the activities under "Exploration of Form in Time and Space" that follow will also help utilize the child's ability to develop ocular control and the visual motor match.

EXPLORATION OF FORM IN SPACE AND TIME

The child is still exploring self and he will be giving his attention to any movement that he is in the process of learning. As each new movement becomes automatic; that is, when he no longer has to think about the "how" of moving a part or combination of parts, his attention will shift to the result of his movements. He will begin to observe the relationships between himself and objects and the relationships within and between objects.

All children learn more adequately when activities are planned in such a way that part of the time the child must adapt to the teacher's presentation and at other times he is allowed free play periods when he can choose what he wants to do. Thus he has an opportunity to develop what Piaget calls equilibruim. Equilibrium is a balance between accommodation and assimilation, and the child is constantly struggling to develop such a balance.

Through imitation, compliance with verbal directions or commands, and adapting to group rules the child accommodates himself to external realities and assimilation is subbordinated to accommodation.

In free play the child makes the environment adapt to his own wishes; thus accommodation is subordinated to assimilation.

In the child with learning disabilities we often find a lack of equilibrium. He either takes over and attempts to make his whole environment adapt to his wishes or depends totally on others to shape his world and his life. Neither type of child faces reality. One is a dictator and the other a nonentity. Neither is well adjusted or happy.

As you work with the child use the appropriate names for the object and term for the activity you wish the child to learn. Make sure that your verbalization and the child's attention or action occur simultaneously in time.

1. Say "in" when the child is in the box, or as the object enters the container.
2. Make sure his eyes are on the object you are naming.

If the child is having difficulty understanding verbal presentations and/or translating them into a motor or verbal output, check your presentation. Possibly you are talking too fast, using too many words, or not giving him time to translate (see "Learning to Speak and Communicate—Receptive Language," this section, and "Behavior Control, Pre-Readiness, Second Level").

Plan activities so that the child can observe, explore and interact with the following relationships.

EXPLORATION OF SELF

The child continues to learn about his own body, its movements and parts. Use the suggestions under "Exploration of Body" in Stage II and emphasize the following parts:

neck	knees	ankles
shoulders	toes	chin
elbows	fingers	cheek
hips	wrists	forehead

MOVEMENTS *vs* NON-MOVEMENT

1. Of self: start, move, stop (see Movement Control)
2. Of objects: child as the mover

THE CONSTRUCTS OF OBJECTS

1. Continue to encourage the child to use tactual-kinesthetic, visual, auditory and olfactory means of exploring objects in his environment. He should have opportunities to use each sense independently and two or more in various combinations.
2. Supply a variety of objects that will encourage (a) use of each hand, (b) use of both hands simultaneously, and (c) use of his arms.
3. Occasionally present an object in reverse of the way it is to be used to make sure the child is aware of the workable end of the object; for example: present a spoon, hammer, screw driver in reverse position or cup or glass up side down.

IMITATION

1. Present opportunities for the child to imitate the movement of two body parts, simultaneously and in sequence.
2. Encourage imitation of social activities.
3. Have child imitate movement, manipulation and placement of objects.

OBJECT PERMANENCE

1. As the child watches, hide an object randomly under one of two separate covers. He is to remove the correct cover and find the object. Use pieces of cloth, inverted tin cans or opaque plastic container as covers.
2. Hide the object under one of three covers.
3. Hide it under three superimposed covers. The teacher might cover the object with a small tin can, then a larger one over that and finally a third one.
4. Play simple games of hide-and-seek.

TRAJECTORY OF OBJECT

1. Have the child drop, roll and throw for the fun of the activity; when it goes well, encourage him to follow the object with his eyes
2. Have him follow with his eyes when an object is dropped or rolled by another.
3. In each of these activities use a variety of objects of different weight from bean bags to feathers.

CONTAINER AND CONTAINED

1. Self and Container

Children begin learning about the amount of space they occupy by experimenting with putting themselves into contained spaces. Supply boxes, barrels, cupboards, shelves that the child can get into. Some should be too big, some too small and some should be a size he can fit into snugly and in a variety of positions.

2. Object and Container

A variety of containers and things that can be put in and taken out should be supplied—also a few things that will not fit into a given container. For example: pails, cans, boxes, simple peg boards with large pegs, blocks, spools, pebbles, balls, sand and water.

TRANSPORTING

1. Require the child to transport objects, large and small.
   a. Supply large objects—hard and soft blocks, chairs, stuffed toys, wheeled toys, boxes, etc.
   b. Encourage the child to carry, drag, pull, push.
   c. Encourage him to do these actions on hands and knees, on knees, or when walking.

2. Obstacle courses

Require the child to move and manipulate his whole body through a variety of obstacle courses.

   a. He should have to wiggle, squirm, crawl, creep and climb; through, over, under, in, out, between and behind a variety of obstacles.
   b. Obstacles—pieces of furniture, ladders, tires, boards, tunnels (different sizes).
   c. The obstacles should be separated at first. As soon as he can master three or four, arrange them close together along a course, so the child must make a variety of postural changes as he moves through them.

RECEIPT AND PROPULSION

1. Introduce games that require the child to:
   a. Pass objects to another person.
   b. Catch an object rolled across the floor to him.
   c. Roll an object to another person.
   d. Drop objects into a large container.
   e. Throw objects into a large container.

CAUSALITY

Supply toys that have casual mechanisms; for example, wind up mechanism, push down levers, toys that need to be turned or tipped to get a given result.

A child whose overall performance is at this level may grasp the hand of the person who presented the toy and move it toward the mechanism suggesting that the other person make it work, or he may hand it back and indicate by gesture or word that he wants the other person to make it work.

A child at a higher perceptual level may endeavor to solve the problem but if he fails he may use the approach above. It is best to encourage the child to give it a try before helping him. If he cannot do it, place his hands in the proper positions and manipulate his hands to get the desired results.

MEANS TO AN END

1. Present the child who has taken an object in each hand with a third object to see how he will react. The earliest development reaction is to put one down to take the third. Later he should transfer one to other hand (if they are small enough that he can hold two in one hand), then take third.
2. Place objects out of reach but on a second object that is within reach. Child should pull the supporting object to self in order to reach desired object. Example: toy or piece of food on a sheet of paper, cardboard, piece of cloth and so on.
3. Require various forms of locomotion to gain desired object (child must be able to move well enough that he can keep his mind on the goal).
4. Present opportunities where child must work out a way to obtain an object that is out of reach unless he uses an extension of his body (chair, box, etc.) or extension of his arm, such as a stick. Don't give verbal cues.

SIGNALS AND SIGNS

The child should be able to foresee an event conceived as independent of his own action but connected with the action of an object or another person. He begins to call upon memory and retention. Early signs are: refusal of an activity he had not enjoyed previously and awareness of the next step in the daily schedule. Soon after he should begin to anticipate results based on a generalization, or maybe it would be more adequate to say an over-generalization of earlier experiences.

For example: The child who has experienced the stickiness of bread and peanut butter may look at his fingers after touching a picture of it; if he has learned to say "bless you" when another person sneezes, he will also say it if they cough, or if he is frightened by a dog he is frightened by all dogs or even a picture of a dog.

chapter 6

Learning to Speak
and Communicate

The child continues to sort out and combine the multiple movement possibilities of his tongue, lips and jaws. As he does so, more sounds become possible. As he perfects the movements he attends less to the movement and more to the resultant sounds until sound making, sound matching and sound imitation become exciting games. He experiments with variations of pitch, volume, rhythm and combinations of sounds. He repeats them over and over until they occur automatically with the same inflection and emphasis that he will use later when speaking in sentences.

The beginning of expressive language occurs as the child imitates first his own sounds, then those of others. He also uses sounds to accompany his gestures and actions. In this manner the child conveys his needs and desires.

For the child who is still experiencing difficulty with sound making, imitation and application of the social language of his environment, it will be necessary to continue to emphasize relaxation and it may be wise to look for other interfering factors.

MOVEMENT

To speak, a child must differentiate many fine, intricate movements of his tongue, larynx, lips and jaws, then control and coordinate them.

All goes well if he does not encounter too many interferences or the same interferences over too long a period of time. Body tension can interfere with the differentiation of any or all movements. Persistent head conjestion due to allergies, colds or other infections can interfere with breathing through the nose. Such a child will breathe through his mouth and fail to develop adequately differentiated lip and jaw movements.

For some children many of the movements may have been differentiated in early childhood but at a later date they fell into disuse, because of one of the interferences listed above. The amount of movement therapy which will be needed will depend on how completely the interfering factors can be eliminated. If the allergies, infections and tension can be relieved and their relief maintained, far less time will need to be spent on differentiation, coordination and control and the possibility of the child maintaining and integrating the new movements is far greater.

We have already discussed the importance of stomach relaxation and adequate breathing for speech. Shoulder relaxation has been emphasized as a pre-requisite for gross motor differentiation; it is also needed for adequate speech.

It also may be necessary to see that the child's neck, face, jaw, and lips are without tension. Use atypical positioning and massage to eliminate tension in the neck and deep massage and manipulation to relax the face, jaws and lips.

No recommendations for movement training will be given here since they were covered in detail in a previous publication by Chaney and Kephart, *Perceptual Training* (Chapter 8, p. 123).

IMITATION OF MOVEMENTS

As soon as the child is aware of and can make a movement of his tongue, lips and jaw, encourage him to imitate you as you make single movements and series of movements. First make just the movements, then the movement with sounds; do not, however, discourage the child if he makes sounds with his movements.

LISTENING

Sometimes a child learns adequately during the babbling and jargon stages because the demand for specific isolation and combination of sounds is minimal. He develops a good internal language, but has difficulty imitating and using the social language of his environment.
The interfering factors may be:

1. A minimal hearing loss at the level at which speech sounds are received.
2. Intermittent interferences to hearing, due to allergies, head colds, infections which prevent him from receiving consistent input (the words spoken by others don't always sound the same). This in turn results in poor integration and output (his imitation does not match or maybe does not even resemble the input).
3. Feedback of his own voice is distorted because of the distorted output and because he does not always hear his own voice in the same way.

Thus the child does not hear the same word in the same way often enough to isolate it and make it his own. When speaking, the words come out differently each time he uses them and are often not recognizable to the listener. Because his words are not recognized, he receives no positive reinforcement and finally quits using oral language and relies instead on gestures and the few words he was able to isolate for communication. Such a child becomes more and more dependent on his visual-motor processes for learning and ceases to attend auditorily.

To remedy:

1. Remove the interfering factors if at all possible; that is, clear up the allergies or infections, or correct the hearing loss.
2. Accent the auditory input through amplification, earphones, and/or de-amplification, whispering.
3. De-emphasize the visual input or at least make sure that the visual input is directly and specifically matched to the auditory input. The visual can be de-emphasized by having the child close his eyes or wear a comfortable blindfold while listening. To match the visual to the auditory make sure the child's eyes are attending to what you are naming or describing. Reinforce this by introducing kinesthetic/tactual stimuli—take the child's hand and have him point directly to what you are naming or have him feel, manipulate or imitate what you are describing.

Another child may not attend auditorily because he knows he will not understand or be able to perform as expected. A third may be so involved kinesthetically or visually that he hears but does not integrate. A fourth may become too involved in his own private world, which for him is more comfortable that the outside world which is always asking too much of him. Still another may hear clearly but be incapable of, or too slow at, translating the auditory input into vocal or motor output; or if the presentation is too long or elaborate, he may lose the context or the sequence; if so, his responses are incorrect and he soon learns that it is safer not to respond at all for thus he avoids being looked upon as the dummy.

When working with the child who does not attend auditorily it is necessary to analyze each child's difficulties and find out why he is not attending before making verbal presentations.

The following suggestions should be helpful.

1. Make sure that what you are asking is within the child's capabilities; that is, he can perform without excessive stress or effort.
2. Check to see if hypertension is interfering.
3. Make sure you have his visual attention. If his eyes are focused elsewhere, the chances are that his attention is also focused elsewhere.
4. Speak slowly and distinctly and use simple, unelaborated verbal presentations.
5. Once a statement is made or a direction given, *wait,* give the child time to translate it and act. As the child becomes more adept, the waiting period can be shortened.
6. Do not permit him to initiate action until you have finished giving directions. Movement may interfere with auditory attention, particularly if his movements are not automatic (if he must attend to and direct them).
7. Ask the child to repeat what you have said before putting it into action.

LEARNING TO LISTEN AND ACT ON WORDS

These tasks may be easily adapted to the classroom by having the children take turns.

1. Several times a day, have the children play a game of being quiet and relaxed with eyes shut. The voice and the whole body should be still. Each child should assume the position in which he is most comfortable and relaxed (lying on the floor, seated in a chair, semi supine against the wall, etc.). At first it may not be possible to maintain this quietness for more than two seconds, but after a few weeks it may be extended to two or three minutes.
2. Once the child can maintain reasonable quiet for fifteen seconds or more, whisper his name and have him rise quietly and come to you. At first, it will be necessary to re-introduce the quiet relaxation after he has been called. As the child's listening ability improves, give him commands in the same whispered voice and position yourself in various areas of the room—near, far, in front of him and behind him.

3. To further encourage the child to listen and at the same time prevent yourself from falling into the habit of out-shouting him, make a habit of using a low quiet tone of voice when presenting food, tasks or play items that he enjoys.

SOUND MAKING

The elaboration of sounds and the speaking of words presupposes the ability to listen and auditorily discriminate sounds, the ability to look and visually discriminate mouth movements, control the speech mechanism, control breathing, and, finally, imitate the sounds of others.

SOUNDS FOR FUN

1. Games
   a. Talk to the child using a combination of gestures and repetious, continuous sounds, i.e., jargon. Encourage the child to answer back in the same manner. He is not to repeat your series of sounds, but to answer with his own. The fun increases if several children and the teacher are involved.
   b. Play a simple tune and encourage the child to "sing" using his own sounds, words or combination of sounds and words.
   c. Encourage the child to match sounds to his movements as he plays, i.e., ah-ah-ah as he rocks and so on. Only vocalizations maintained over time can give the throat, larynx, tongue, jaw and lips the exercise which will prepare them for the later speaking of sentences.
      (1) Quiet sounds to slow quiet movements.
      (2) Loud sounds to boisterious movements.
      (3) Say what he is doing as he moves a body part: up-down, out-back, etc.

IMITATIONS OF SOUNDS

1. Encourage the child to imitate:
   a. Single sounds
   b. Repetitous sounds
   c. Combination sounds
2. The teacher should present the sounds slowly and distinctly as she exaggerates her mouth movements to give well-defined visual as well as auditory cues.

3. The following is the order in which vocal imitations usually occur:

    a. Single vowels—eh-uh-ah, etc.

    b. Single syllables —da-ka-ba.

    c. Repetitious same vowels—eh, eh, eh—ah, ah, ah.

    d. Repetitious same syllables—da, da, da—ba, ba, ba.

    e. Facial expressions—frown, grin, pucker lips and kiss, pucker lips and blow, sniff, etc.

    f. Combined syllables—da, ba, ba—a, ba, da.

    g. Words made up of repetitious syllables—dada, mama, byebye, bebe (baby).

    h. Words (echolalia).

COMMUNICATION

SOUNDS, WORDS AND GESTURES

1. Encourage the child to use whatever sounds, words or gestures he is capable of making: to get attention; to express simple needs or desires; to support his rejections. Whatever means he uses should be accepted. Do not tell the child that his method is incorrect. Accept his means of communication, then restate the same communication as you supply his needs. Example: If a child pulls the teacher to the cupboard, then points to the crayons as he makes sounds, the teacher might say, "Do you want the crayons?" Then, as she hands them to him she might say, "Here are the crayons."

2. A child repeats performances that are laughed at and performances that attract attention of any kind. Acts that are responded to with amusement, praise or scolding are apt to be repeated. Be careful, therefore, not to overemphasize in any way that which you would prefer not to have repeated.

3. When communicating with children performing at or below the perceptual motor level, it may be necessary to accompany your verbalization with descriptive gestures, to increase comprehension of the language. As you say "Open the door," demonstrate the act of opening the door, etc.

4. Help the child learn to react to different moods: affection and scolding; happy and sad tones and expressions.

5. Help the child learn to respond to verbal instructions.

    a. No-no (at first he may go ahead and do the forbidden act a few minutes later, but he will learn if you are consistent).

    b. His own name.

    c. Simple verbal commands such as: stand up, close the door, or open the door, sit up, pick up, sit down, turn around, come here, go get, bring me.

These are first introduced with gestures and demonstrations, if necessary. The child really responds to key words and depends on gestures for the rest.

LEARNING THAT THINGS HAVE NAMES

CATEGORIES TO BE USED

1. Self: body parts, familiar foods, familiar clothing.
2. Home: familiar household objects, family members, pet animals.

MAKING THE CHILD AWARE THAT THINGS HAVE NAMES AND CAN BE IDENTIFIED IN MANY WAYS

1. Naming of body parts:

   As you work through the activities of differentiation you will be using tactual, kinesthetic and visual cues for identification, as well as naming, to identify body parts. The child should be able to identify and move each part when named. If he shows any desire to name the part himself, he should be encouraged to do so.
2. Visual exploration of objects:

   a. As the children work or play, move among them and name the object with which each child is playing. Make sure he is attending to the object when you name it.
   b. Place several familiar objects on a table. Pick one up, show it to the children and name it. Ask the children to repeat the name, then pass it around for each to explore.
3. Matching:

   a. Several sets of same objects will be needed, one for each child; if you have only two sets, work individually or divide the second set among the children.
   b. Show and name an object and ask the child or children to find the one like it. As soon as the children understand what they are to do, vary the verbal presentation. Example: Find one like this.
   Give me the one like this.
   Where is the car?
   Point to the soap.

The variations in verbal presentations will help the child generalize so that he need not depend on a single phrase for understanding.

4. Recognition by name:

   a. Name a body part or object and ask the child to find it.

5. Recognition by sound:
   b. Sound an object (out of the child's sight) and have the child identify which object made the sound.

6. Naming:

   a. Present or point to a body part or object and have the children name:
       (1) As a group
       (2) Individually

At first some children may give only the initial sound; accept their answer but reinforce use of the whole word by saying something like, "Yes it is a _____." Accent your pronunciation of the key word.

part 4

Readiness: First Level
Perceptual-Motor Learning

chapter 7

Perceptual-Motor Learning

At the readiness level, perceptual-motor learning will be at its height. The integration of motor, visual and auditory information began with the initial emphasis on the motor data with subsequent visual, tactual or auditory attention to the movement, thus a visual to motor, tactual to motor or auditory to motor match was made. In the Readiness stage the child will experiment with movement and attend primarily to the result of his actions on objects or the result of the movement of a tool, as in the use of a hammer, a screw driver or a crayon.

The child's eyes and ears have become more proficient in supplying information and, in fact, are beginning to take the lead. As the eyes begin to lead, the hand follows along to confirm the result. If trouble or confusion occurs, the child returns to the use of the hand for verification of the information. Thus the transition to a motor to visual match or motor to auditory match occurs.

Unless the perceptual and motor information are related to each other, there will be little or no integration of perceptual information and motor information. Occasionally a child builds up a body of perceptual information by relating percept to percept, but he is not able to relate them to a motor response. Thus, he may read instructions or a passage regarding a game and respond verbally and knowingly about that which he had read, but not be able to perform the tasks described in the reading.

Another child may be unable to carry out instructions. He can repeat them but not act them out. Neither can match perceptual information (either auditory or visual) with motor information. Therefore they cannot

PERCEPTUAL

Although in this curriculum perception is part of the sequence of development and learning, teachers must be aware that its beginnings lie in early sensory awarenss and primitive interpretation of the outside world. As time goes on, the process becomes more complex and develops into an elementary form of perception. Sensory awareness is the first stage of perceptual learning.

Whatever perceptual learning can take place must take place within the limits or capabilities established by the child's receptor-projection organs (vision, audition, kinesthesis, taction, etc.). When working with the child with learning disabilities, however, these "limits" or "capabilities" can frequently be extended via training in sensory motor, motor perceptual and perceptual motor tasks.

Solley and Murphy (1960) state that it is agreed that a physical stimulus must be present and must excite some sense reception on receptors before perception occurs. It is important that the child's attention to the stimulus continue over time in order that the perception of one object can be compared with that of another (manipulations and comparisons of similarities, differences). These manipulations and comparisons of similarities and differences in the motor perceptual and perceptual motor stages prepare the child for perceptual learning.

Greatly simplified, perception is the ability to recognize and be aware of relationships. However, it is not necessary to understand these relationships. The child perceives that this picture is similar to or different from that picture or knows that this movement (which is kinesthetic perception) is the same as or different from that movement, before he can describe how it is similar or different. The initial perception of what is different and significant about an object is necessary to the further perception of all its elements and their relationships. The learning and matching of several distinctive features and their transfer from one sense avenue to the other develops percepts; the manipulation and integration of percepts makes conceptual thinking possible.

The Readiness child enjoys games and tasks that challenge him to utilize his balancing mechanism, a variety of locomotion patterns and finer and finer eye-hand movement.

He will continue to explore and critically examine the permanence and construction of objects, and learn to use familiar objects appropriately.

Space and time elements will attract his attention. Where before he had only vague impressions of space and time as he attended to self and/ or the object, he now begins to isolate specific temporal or spatial aspects of an activity in which he is engaged; that is, he will study nearness and separation, vertical and horizontal alignment, open space *vs* occupied space and enclosure. He will show interest in continuity and noncontinuity as he explores surfaces, edges and angles and study the ordering of objects, actions and events.

Imitation will be at its height and he will learn many of the language symbols that stand for things and actions. The symbols will take on meaning and become signifiers as he uses them to stand for or represent objects, such as a doll represents a child, or a stick becomes a pipe. Words will be used to signify objects, actions and emotions, and imaginative play becomes an important part of his life as he recalls and re-enacts previous experiences.

Size, shape, texture and color will attract his attention. Causality will become an exciting reality as he learns how to manipulate and use more objects in his environment, and he will become the prime mover.

Foresight and problem solving will expand and the child will depend less and less on trial and error. The following activities are suggested for the child who needs to develop or reinforce these percepts.

BALANCE AND LOCOMOTION

During the third level of pre-readiness the child mastered locomotion on his hands and knees and established a walking pattern which may still be unsteady and irregular. The child now must learn to elaborate and to vary these modes of locomotion and learn new ones. This in turn will make increased demands for balance.

The child at this stage of development normally practices and experiments with movement in many ways: on his knees and on his feet, on his hands and feet, on hands and knees. He creeps over, around and under obstacles about the house. He affects a wide base (feet apart) in order to maintain balance in the upright position. He bends over to pick up objects or to open cupboard doors. He carries objects about the house or playground; he squats to play and learns to jump upward, forward, off objects and over low obstacles. At first the jumping movement may involve only an upward motion of the body. If he overestimates the degree of shift of body weight he falls, but his experimentations continue. A youngster experiencing a learning difficulty, however, may not continue to experiment with movement and balance should he fall too often or fail. If his problems are less severe he may learn to maintain his orientation and to move through tension. In either case, activities need to be presented to encourage and help the youngster to experiment. If the tension continues to interfere, then activities to teach relaxation while moving should be introduced.

COORDINATION AND BALANCE

1. With the child on his stomach, have him bend his knees and bring his feet up to buttocks, then reach back and grasp his ankles with his hands. He is to maintain the hold on his ankles as he:
   a. Rolls from side to side.
   b. Rolls to a side, relaxes, then rolls back to center and stops.
   c. Rocks fore and aft.

2. With the child on his back, have him draw both knees up to his chest, then clasp his hands:
   a. Under his thighs.
   b. Over the top of his legs just below his knees.

In each of the positions above have the child:
   a. Roll from side to side.
   b. Rock fore and aft (coming forward to seated position).
   c. Roll to side, relax then back to center and relax.

3. On hands and knees, have him:
   a. Raise and extend a leg out behind him, hold 3 to 5 seconds, then lower. Repeat with the other leg.
   b. As he raises a leg he also raises his head until his eyes are pointed straight ahead, hold, relax and lower both head and leg.
   c. He now lifts head and leg, holds, lowers and touches knee to nose or forehead, holds then repeats several times using slow rhythmic movements.

4. Seated:
   a. On the balance board:
      (1) Seat the child cross-legged on the board so that he can be tipped fore and aft and side to side. His hands should be on his ankles or knees.
      (2) Tip the board, slowly and gently at first; later, more rapidly.
      (3) Do not always maintain the same pattern. The child should "feel" the movement and his own adjustments, not intellectualize the direction of the board and move accordingly.

b. As the child sits on the floor with his legs extended have him:

(1) Straighten then relax his back.

(2) Reach out to touch his toes. The legs are to remain extended as he does so. If he cannot perform, encourage him to rock fore and aft as he continues to reach. Repeat eight or ten times each work session. Then, once fingers and toes make contact and legs remain extended, five times each session will be sufficient.

(a) Have the child seated with legs spread apart and arms at his side. Have him reach out with his right hand toward the toes of his left foot (do not permit the knee to bend), then return arm to beginning position. Repeat several times. If at first he cannot reach his toes, let him hold a stick in his hand and over a period of several weeks, shorten the stick and then remove it.

(b) Have him touch the toes of the right foot with the left hand. Repeat.

(c) Have him touch the toes of the left foot with the right hand, then the toes of the right foot with the left hand. Repeat.

5. In upright position. In order to function efficiently, a child must maintain balance automatically; it must be a "part of him" as the child moves about exploring his environment. Otherwise, he will have to pay attention to the task of remaining upright on his feet. For the classroom child, this could be especially troublesome since so much learning occurs as he goes to and from school, as he participates in gym classes, science exhibits and so forth. The knowledge gained from the experiences will be nullified if he has to attend to balance during this stage of development.

Many of the tasks that follow involve movements of the arms, legs and trunk, in order to teach the children to maintain balance during varying situations. These movements, to be performed easily, require that the children have differentiated those body parts. If the teacher discovers that some children cannot move these limbs individually, work with differentiation is recommended. If the teacher finds that some children cannot move body parts in combination, then work with coordination is indicated (Arms with each other, arms and trunk, arms and legs, etc.).

To help the child who is experiencing difficulty maintaining his balance in an upright posture, present him with simple standing tasks.

a. Standing on a block

(1) Place a block that is at least six inches high on the floor.

(a) Have the child stand still on the block.

(b) He is to change the direction he faces each time he gets up on to the block in order to forestall his learning orientation in only one direction.

This standing task may reveal that some children, when they graduate to the more complex task of standing, shift the job of maintaining balance to their lower backs. This shift creates rigidity through the hips and a posture that is easily recognizable. They are distributing their weight mass atypically around their center of gravity. The first thing to do is to loosen or to relax the hips in order to redistribute the weight mass to its proper position. Refer to tasks involving differentiation of hips, i.e., hip roll.

(c) Next the child is to experiment with different movements of his body parts as he stands on the block.

1) Move his arms in a variety of ways—together and separately; for example: hands on shoulders, out to the side, swing one arm to the rear, swing them alternately as in marching; bend and touch toes; catch and throw balls; pass balls.
2) Move his trunk in a variety of ways: twist from side to side; sway back and forth; bend and rotate from the waist in each direction.
3) Move his legs in a variety of ways: stand on each foot; swing one leg; flex each knee, bringing the knee up as far as possible; move leg out to the side, etc.

b. Kneeling on the block to elaborate the activities, also have the child perform while on his knees.
c. Standing on the floor, the youngsters should stand with their feet approximately twelve inches apart. This wide base will give them more stability as they experiment with the movements in a standing position. The tasks below may be varied by having the children work in their bare feet.

(1) Arm Postures:

Begin by having the children stand quietly with their arms at their sides for ten seconds. Add variations by changing the arm positions. (Hands on hips, hands on head, arms out to the side, etc.) These are all "still" postures.

(2) Leg Postures:

Leg positions may also be varied within the still posture. For example, the children may stand with one foot in front of the other, feet close together, on one foot, one foot raised, knee bent, a leg straight out to the side or straight out in front, etc.

(3) Trunk Movements:

These movements are important because at this time the children are learning about shifting of body weight and what it does to balance. They are also experimenting with space around them.

(a) The children should stand with their feet approximately twelve inches apart, with their hands on their hips. They should bend forward at the waist, then straighten. Repeat five times. Movements to the rear and to the side may also be practiced. Variations of this task may be presented.

(b) Vary the placement of the hands (head, shoulders) and bend.

(c) Sway from the waist, from side to side.

(d) Twist from the waist, from side to side.

(e) All of the above with the hands clasped and extended out in front. The trunk and arms move together.

d. Kneeling balance on the floor.
   Same activities as standing on the floor.

e. Kneeling balance on rocking board.

(1) Rock the board side to side and fore to aft as the child maintains balance.

(2) The child experiments on the board.

f. Standing balance on rocking board.

(1) Rock the board side to side as the child maintains balance.

(2) The child experiments on the board.

g. Standing with arm movements.

(1) The children stand as suggested earlier and move their arms in a variety of patterns while maintaining posture without swaying or tension.

(2) Vary the tempo from slow to fast.

(a) Arms extended out in front with hands clasped together, swing arms from side to side.

(b) Arms extended straight up over the head, hands clasped,

move the arms forward until they touch the body, then up and back as far as they will go. Repeat. (Keep the arms straight at all times.)

(c) Extend the arms out to the sides at shoulder level. Bring first one arm across the body to touch the shoulder of the opposite arm, then repeat with the other; continue for six counts.

(d) Introduce circular movements of each arm, both together and alternating. Circular movements may be made while the arms are extended out to the side, in front, down at the side or up over the head.

(e) Circular movements may be made by rotating the arms and shoulder to the rear as well as forward. Children who are tense will experience the most difficulty with the movement to the rear. Vary the circular movements by varying the size of the circles.

  h. Kneeling with arm movements—same as above.
  i. Standing with leg movements:

(1) There are many variations of leg movements ranging from simple individual movements to alternating movements. Have the children stand with their feet about three inches apart, then slide one leg forward or out to the side and back. Repeat five times, then perform with other leg.

(2) Swing a leg back and forth from the hip. At first ask for only a short range of movement in each direction. Likewise, one movement in each direction is a good place to start. Both the range of movements and the number of movements may be increased as the children become more accustomed to rather rapid changes in shifts of body weight. Should this task have to be simplified, the child may swing his leg forward then back to the standing position, rest briefly, then swing it back and then go to the rest position again. Have the child perform with each leg.

(3) The movements above should also be adapted to lifting the leg out to the side.

(4) Have them move both legs.

(a) Stoop and stand: Have the child stoop, hold for two to six seconds, then stand, hold and repeat. Prevent forward tilt of upper body and discourage very deep knee bends for they interfere with the jumping pattern.

(b) Jumping up and down. The child is to jump, rest and balance, then jump again. If the child has worked through the activities of the previous stages he should have no difficulty working through the jumping patterns. However, there may be some old interfering habits of movements that need to be corrected.

One child may go through the jumping movements but his feet fail to leave the floor. This may be due to improper body position, improper leg action or failure to coordinate the rest of his body into the task. To correct:

1. Practice body position and leg action in the stoop.
2. Lightly grasp his sides and, as he thrusts up with his legs, lift gently to bring his body into the air. Gradually provide less and less lift.
3. Hold his hands and jump with him or have two children jump together.
4. Encourage the child to jump alone.

Another child may be able to get his feet off the floor but his leg action is improper. Such a child stoops then thrusts upward with the legs to lift the body, but the legs immediately flex and, as the downward move begins, he thrusts his legs downward, and the feet slap the floor as they land.

Grasp the child's wrists lightly. Ask the child to squat down, not too far. From this starting position, ask him to thrust with his legs until he is upright and hold the upright position with his legs straight. At this point he is not to leave the ground. When this thrust and hold has been mastered, ask him to thrust upward with more force. This additional force will carry his body free of the ground. Be sure he keeps his legs stiff after the thrust. This will cause him to land stiff legged but you can work out the landing pattern, as will be discussed later, after the take-off pattern has been learned.

Sometimes a child is unable to use both sides of the body equally. He pushes off more strongly with one leg than the other and in landing, one foot strikes the floor ahead of the other. This problem is frequently related to lack of differentiation of one side of the body, and the differentiation and coordination tasks of previous stages should be worked through first.

When you return to the jumping, have the child stand with his feet farther apart than normal when he jumps. This position makes a unilateral jump more difficult since the weight must be shifted further before pushing off.

In the landing, call the child's attention to the sound produced when his feet hit the floor. Ask him to make just one sound, not two, when he lands.

An additional problem in landing is presented by the child who cannot coordinate the flexion of ankle, knee and hip to take up the shock.

This child lands stiff legged and inflexibly. Often verbal explanation and visual demonstration are sufficient to permit him to learn the proper pattern.

A trampoline is very useful in working through this problem since the results of jumping stiff legged and with legs flexed are greater. This fact gives the child a clearer knowledge of results. The entire motion is also slower, giving the child a chance to observe and experiment with his responses. The action of knees and ankles can be emphasized by teaching the child to stop. In order to stop, the knees are bent to take up the spring of the canvas. The contrast between the stopping response and the normal jumping response calls the child's attention to the leg action involved. In the absence of a trampoline, bed springs and mattresses offer a partial substitute.

LOCOMOTION AND BALANCE—CLASSROOM ACTIVITIES

Creeping

1. Encourage the child to use creeping as a means of locomotion. Have him creep on his hands and knees across the room and under and around the desks.
2. Place obstacles in his path which will demand that he go up and over. A device young children love is a combination stairs and slide. (Creative Play Things), but boxes, wastebaskets, etc. may also be used.
3. Place a plank that is at least twelve inches wide upon two supports that are four inches in height. The child may now creep from one end to the other forward and then backwards.
4. Remove one support so that the plank is inclinded; again the child should creep forward up the board. He may come down backward or forward. As the youngster becomes more adept in managing himself, the angle of incline may be increased.
5. At any time during his work on the above tasks, a request may be made for the child to stay perfectly still. It is often harder for the child to "balance" in the still position than while moving. To some extent momentum assists the child in his maintenance of balance, whereas being still requires a greater degree of control of body parts.

Upright Posture

Locomotion comprises those activities by which the child moves through space. His knowledge of overall space and of the relationships between objects in space, beyond arm's reach, develops out of exploration through locomotion. To gather systematic knowledge of his spatial relationships, however, requires that the child attend to his explorations, not to his movements. It is therefore necessary that locomotor activities be sufficiently varied and efficient to permit all the kinds of movement necessary to all types of spatial exploration without the necessity of diverting attention from the exploration to the process of exploring.

A great many children with learning disability show deficiencies in locomotion. When they walk, they stalk along with feet spread apart; the limbs move stiffly and sluggishly or their movements may be taut with extreme tension in all limbs, resulting in short, explosive locomotor movements which are difficult to control. When they approach an obstacle they may pause and appear to have to "think out" what to do next. Their movements do not flow freely nor are they sufficiently well coordinated to permit the child to explore space. Their repertoire of locomotor movements is so small that they are always in trouble when locomotion is essential to the development of information.

The locomotions to be mastered at this time are walking, running and jumping.

Each act of locomotion requires balance. If the child's balancing patterns are inadequate or faulty he must then attend to balance as well as locomotion, and learning while moving becomes impossible. Examples: The child whose problem involves balance as well as locomotion is the one who starts out walking, picks up momentum until he is running and does not stop until he runs into something, stumbles and falls. If a child is accustomed to maintaining static balance by fixating his eyes on a given point in his environment, he will become disoriented and lose his balance as he moves through space.

Variations

The child who has mastered balance, differentiation, coordination and locomotion as presented in the previous section of this curriculum should have no difficulty with the following variations which are designed to help eliminate habitual, inadequate locomotion patterns in an upright posture and give multiple and varied opportunities for experimentation with balance, coordination and locomotion.

Should a child experience difficulty with the following activities, analyze the problem and isolate the interfering factors. Go back to the previous section for necessary remedial work.

1. Vary the presentation of tasks

    a. Imitation (vision).
    b. Verbal instructions (audition).
    c. Kinesthetic awareness (move the youngster through a desired movement; he may be blindfolded).

2. Use specific tasks for specific problems.

   a. Tight heel cords (interfere with flexible movement).

      (1) Refer to Relaxation of Foot and Leg and work with the ankle as specified.

      (2) Experiment with variations of walking patterns—i.e., walk with knees bent (back straight), heel-toe walk, etc.

   b. Hyper-extended legs (interferes with flexible movement, awareness of movement)

      (1) Walk with knees bent.

      (2) Swim using flutter kick.

      (3) Alleviate tension of cords at back of leg.

   c. Exaggerated use of knee (Action of the knee forces lower leg movement out in back. Compensates for poor coordination of leg, lack of differentiation of hips).

      (1) Holding chair and swinging leg from hip.

      (2) Walking with legs stiff swinging from hip.

      (3) Same as above in water.

      (4) Kicking in water—hold ankles so child must move whole leg (may have to move to thigh).

   d. Forced walking for the child who leans forward using the weight of the upper body to propel him forward.

      (1) Have the child stand, facing away from a second person. The other person puts a towel, rope or belt around the child's chest, then holds on to both ends. He tells the child to walk forward as he gently and steadily pulls back on the "reins."

      (2) Encourage the child to move his leg at the hip as he walks.

      (3) Discourage any bending forward, thus pulling with the chest.

   e. For the child who tilts his upper trunk backward and thrusts forward with the leg as he walks. The child faces toward the other person. Put the "reins" around the back of his chest and have him walk backward against resistance.

   f. Use marching to encourage more hip and knee flexibility in walking.

(1) Play marching games. Encourage the child to lift his knees high in front of him. Use the resistive "reins" if necessary.

(2) Vary the walking patterns. Have the child take short steps, take long steps, slide, leap, cross one leg over another and so on.

(3) Combine arm movements with walking (see "Arm Movements while Standing" for suggestions).

(4) Vary the activity. Have the children walk in a circle, follow one another, randomly, backward, forward, sideways.

(5) Introduce directional, pace and rhythmic changes.

LOCOMOTION AND BALANCE—PLAYGROUND ACTIVITIES

A playground with free form objects, swings, etc. serves as a good environment for experimenting with balance. Let the children work out as many of their balance problems as they can by themselves. Help those who hold back by determining what their difficulty is, and then by using the available equipment to teach them.

1. Problems that may occur during playground activities:

   a. A loss of visual (spatial) orientation.
   b. Difficulty with forward and backward movement.
   c. Poor tactual-kinesthetic awareness.
   d. Poor control of body parts.
   e. Lack of coordination of body parts.
   f. Faulty depth perception.

2. Examples of training activities that may help the youngster overcome the problems listed:

   a. Dealing with a large amount of open and unfamiliar space coupled with a shaky orientation to gravity may cause a youngster to lose himself; i.e., if he is playing with equipment on which he can change direction he may not realize his head is down or his feet are up or which was the direction of his movement. Provide him with a vertical visual target (a tree, fence, slide, etc.). Call his attention to it repeatedly as he moves. Verbalize his position. Work with seated balance, swaying, etc. (as outlined in Pre-Readiness Stage III), both blindfolded and with his eyes on a target.

   b. Many times, because a child uses vision almost exclusively to aid him, the concept of back (behind) is inadequate; thus he cannot move to the rear. Should he attempt this movement he may lose his balance, so unfamiliar is this direction to him, or he may compensate by turning to watch where he is going. Forward movement may be similarly affected. Should the child's visual attention be attracted elsewhere he will lose his balance and fall. Therefore, tasks to strengthen kinesthetic awareness and practice with fore and aft movement in a variety of surroundings will aid him to maintain balance in the preceeding situations. (Refer to Readiness Stages, I, II and III.)

c. Some children do not have a "feel" or awareness of touch. Information usually transmitted by the feet as they touch the ground, for instance, may be lacking or minimal. Therefore, standing balance may be precarious because of this minimal awareness. The same sort of thing happens to children who seem to be always tense or tight or always very loose. These youngsters may lose their balance while crossing irregular terrain or while up on apparatus that requires changes in position. They cannot quickly re-adjust a rigid response pattern to meet the demands of a new situation and they tumble or wobble because of too much tension or not enough tonus in the needed limb to support them. The teacher must then work to increase tactual awareness by having the children perform barefooted.

d. Many children whose movements lack control and coordination are observed on the playground. Arms and legs seemingly move independently of other body parts or remain rigid as other body parts move. Parts of arms may function out of harmony with the rest of the arm. The same observations may be made of the legs. These irregular, often unpredicted movements will serve to interrupt or throw the child off balance. If these problems are noted, it may be necessary to work on the arm and leg differentiation and coordination activities (Pre-readiness II and III, Readiness I).

e. Perception plays a role in a child's orientation to gravity and to space around him. If functioning properly, vision will help to tell the child how far down the ground is, how long a log is, how fast a swing moves, whether or not to step on a stone. If these perceptions are inconsistent or erroneous the child will make incorrect judgements and balance will be disturbed. Because he cannot tell how far down the ground is, he may become frightened, and lose control of body parts and balance. The child at this time relies upon the coordination of two sets of information: visual and kinesthetic. The basis for working in this area lies in Pre-Readiness I, II and III (i.e., obstacle course, creeping up and down stairs, eyehand, eye, foot and so on).

Variation of position

The following are suggestions which may be elaborated upon by the teacher. When utilizing any of these suggestions, a child's well being should be kept in mind. Safety is an important lesson to teach because a child with learning disabilities often may not be able to exercise the proper judgement regarding safe and unsafe or the proper time and place.

1. When moving on a horizontal, inclined or curved surface:
   a. On stomach, back, hands and knees—moving forward, backward, and sideways.
   b. Rolling.
   c. Various position of arms and legs.

2. Movement on a resilient surface (stretched canvas, inner tube, tire, old mattress, supported planks):
   a. The child is bounced in all positions from stomach and back to standing.
   b. The child bounces himself in the various positions.
   c. Child turns as he bounces.
   d. He coordinates arm movements and leg movements.

Refer to *Motoric Aids to Perceptual Training* and *Learning through Individualized Trampoline Activities*.

Using Playground Aparatus

1. Propelling self on a moving object (see "Movement through Space" under "Math Readiness," I).
2. Movement on anchored aparatus.

Playground equipment presents a fine opportunity for children to experience and experiment with balance. Although frowned upon on many playgrounds, walking up one end of a see-saw and then down the other side as the board shifts is an excellent balancing experience.

Children love to experiment, as evidenced by their standing on swings, walking up slides, etc., activities all prohibited for safety reasons. However, the "new look" in playground equipment presents safe opportunities for this kind of "play" with balance and movement.

Summary: The balancing tasks presented overlap into the area of co-ordination. In order for the youngster to coordinate his body parts in the upright posture, he must know and feel how to maintain balance automatically. More complex movement patterns will be presented in future sections.

LEARNING TO WORK RELAXED

MOVEMENT AND RELAXATION (SEATED)

No special equipment is needed to teach relaxation in the classroom. The child sits at a desk or in a chair, with his feet resting comfortably on the floor and his arms hanging limply at his sides. He should sit back in the chair so that the chair back helps him to maintain balance, and his feet should rest comfortably on the floor. This position is designed to reduce the balance problem. Be sure the trunk is straight up and down so that the weight masses are distributed symmetrically around the center of gravity and that the buttocks, not the lower back, carry all the weight of the upper trunk.

1. The teacher stands behind the child, places a hand on either side of his head, and with a firm grip, gently tilts it backward until his face is facing toward the ceiling. If tenseness develops in the neck as the head is moved backward, stop the movement and manipulate the neck muscles until the tenseness is removed, then continue the motion.

    a. To remove tenseness in the neck muscles, hold the head with one hand and place your other hand at the side of the neck with fingers extended and rock the muscle back and forth until the tension is relieved. Manipulate the muscles on one side of the neck first. Then repeat this manipulation on the other side of the neck until each relaxes. If necessary, prop the child's head against your chest and, using both hands, manipulate the muscles on both sides of the neck simultaneously until the head is loose and supported only by your chest.

    b. Continue this procedure until the head can be bent back in this loose and unsupported fashion throughout the extent of the movement. The head should be back far enough so that the line of sight is directed at a point on the ceiling directly above the child's body. Return the head to the upright position supporting it throughout the course of the movement. Be sure the neck muscles remain relaxed.

        (1) If tenseness develops in the neck muscles, stop the movement and manipulate the muscles as before until the tension is relieved.

    c. When the head can be moved without undue tension, ask the child to move his own head forward until his chin rests on his chest.

        (1) Remain in the position behind him so that you can provide support immediately if he gets into trouble.

(2) Be sure the muscles not directly involved in the movement remain relaxed. The head should move forward smoothly and in a controlled manner. It should not fall of its own weight when its center of gravity moves forward off its base, nor should it move out of tension.

(3) Stop his head and relax the neck muscles if tension occurs.

(4) Ask the child to control his head and move it more slowly if it falls.

d. Ask the child to lift his head up to the upright position. This movement is more difficult since the head must be raised against the pull of gravity.

(1) Place your hands on the child's shoulders to keep them relaxed. Observe the cords at the side of the neck. These frequently stand out when undue tension develops. In the event of such tension, stop the movement and restore support by letting him rest his head on your hands. Release the tension by manipulation of the muscles, if necessary. Ask the child to continue the movement.

e. Now ask the child to move his own head backward. Provide support and massage if needed but encourage the child to perform without support. It is more difficult for the child to raise the head to the upright position from the backward angle than it is from the forward angle.

f. When you have worked through the fore and aft movements two or three times, support the head by placing your hands on each side of the face, and gently push the head over until it rests close to the child's shoulder. Watch for tension on the side away from the movement. Observe particularly whether the cords on that side of the neck stand out. If so, manipulate the muscles until the tension is released.

(1) Move the head back to the upright position and continue moving until the opposite side of the head rests close to the shoulder.

(2) Ask the child to perform this movement without your support; keep tension out of those muscles not required in the movement, either through massage or through verbal suggestion to the child should tension continue. If necessary, massage the tight muscles. Have the child continue the movement when relaxed.

(3) The hand should move smoothly through the movement, not flop onto the shoulder as gravity begins to affect the movement, nor catch at any point in between.

2. Since the position of the head is intimately related to the relation-ship of gravity and the maintenance of upright posture, tension fre-quently develops in the arms and legs as the head is moved. Because of the "body follows the head" principle, head movements may cause undue righting or balancing responses. Therefore, it is necessary to check the effect of these head movements on the development of tension in the legs and arms.

   a. It may be necessary to take hold of the arms and shake them gently until they relax. Ask the child to check his legs and place them in a relaxed position before returning to the task. The knees should be slightly apart and the feet resting on the floor.

   With arms and legs relaxed, rotate the child's head to one side until his chin touches his shoulder. Watch for tension in the neck muscles and observe the cords of the neck. If tension develops, manipulate the muscles, as before.

   (1) Turn it to the other side. Frequently tension develops in the lower jaw as the head is moved. The child appears to "lead with his jaw" and pull his head with it or he tightens his jaw, making the head immobile.

   (a) If the jaw tightens as above, tilt the child's head forward and grasp the chin between your thumb and fingers and gently move it back and forth. Encourage the child to re-lax the jaw until you can manipulate it freely in this man-ner. Keep in mind this movement is very slight. After the jaw relaxes, again move his head in both directions.

   b. When you can move his head without any show of tension, ask the child to move his head back and forth slowly; watch for ten-sion. If tension again develops, stop the movement, relax the tense area, then ask him to move again. When he can move his own head help him learn to relax his shoulders.

3. Place your hands over his shoulders with your fingers across the shoulder blades. Gently move the shoulders forward and backward. Verbally encourage the child to relax. Continue until the shoulders are flexible.

   a. If tension develops in the arms, this tension will involve the shoulders and will prevent the flexible movement which is the goal of the activity. Therefore, watch the arms closely and, if they become tense, stop and release the tension before continuing.

   b. Watch for tension in the neck. The chin should not jut out. The head should not move with the shoulders, and the neck should re-main pliable taking up the motion generated in the shoulders.

Keep the feet and legs relaxed and watch for undue tension in the thighs.

c. Next, gently move the child's shoulders up and down with your hands placed on his upper arms. There should be no resistance to the movement of the shoulders. They should move freely. The movement should not flow over into other parts. Watch for tension in the arms, legs and thighs as before.

d. With your hands in the same position, combine the preceding movements rotating the shoulders upward and forward, downward and back; then reverse the direction. Flow-over into other body parts or undue tension should not occur.

e. When the shoulders are relaxed, have the child raise each arm out to the side until they are in a straight line with his shoulders. Grasp them gently; have the child relax them into your hands as you move them in a circular direction. The child's shoulders should be the circle's center. Begin with very small circles and gradually increase in size.

   (1) The shoulder should not "hunch" to accommodate the movement, but should remain relaxed. The head should not thrust forward or backward. The wrists should not stiffen during the movement. They should move with the arm. Coordination of wrist, arm and shoulder is very important in activities such as writing.

   (2) Finally, ask the child to perform these movements for himself without your assistance. Watch for tension in any part and at any phase of the movement. If such tension occurs, perform the same manipulations as before until it is released.

Although the preceding exercises can be expected to achieve movement out of relaxation and kinesthetic figure-ground for the child, it may occasionally be found that tension is still present in the abdominal muscles. If this appears to be the case, first check to be sure that this tension is not being induced by incomplete relaxation of the shoulder or hips. If the apparent tension in the abdomen results from the spread of tension from the shoulder, further work on the neck and shoulders is indicated.

When the child has learned to move out of relaxation, he must learn to make voluntary or constructive responses without the development of tension in those parts of the body not directly involved in the task. Frequently, in an effort to control a constructive response, the child tenses much of the musculature of his body. Instead of aiding control, this excessive effort causes over-control and prevents the precision of movement needed to perform a finely differentiated task. He thus finds himself in a vicious cycle in which he develops additional tension each time he attempts to control his movements. In turn the tension prevents the finer control he is attempting to achieve. He then becomes frustrated and responds with more tension and force, causing his movements to become more explosive and uncontrolled. The harder he tries, the greater his failure.

The solution to this problem lies in reversing the cycle. The child must be taught that, when he wants control, he should relax rather than tense. Once the child knows what relaxation is, how to recognize it and how it can improve movement responses, he can be taught to use this information in the solutions of his problems. He will need to be taught how to make constructive movements out of relaxation and how this procedure helps him control his responses. To move adequately, one must relax prior to movement, then contraction and movement occurs followed again by relaxation, establishing a rhythmic cycle. Tonus as opposed to kinesthetic hypertension is present during a movement.

RELAXATION WHILE ATTENDING TO VISUAL INFORMATION

Have the child seated as before and present a visual target directly in front of him and about 18 inches from his eyes. The target should demand visual attention and recognition; for example, small pictures, letters or numbers pasted on four sides of a penlight, pencil or dowel. Turn the object frequently so that the visual tasks of attention and recognition continue to be demanding. Move the target back and forth from side to side before the child's eyes and ask him to tell you which picture, letter, etc. he sees. Help the child remain relaxed as he pursues the target with his eyes (not his head). If he cannot maintain relaxation while using his eyes return to the ocular and ocular-motor training in the Pre-Readiness sections, keeping him relaxed as he performs. When success is achieved, reintroduce the tasks above.

RELAXATION AND VISUAL-MOTOR TASKS

1. Have the child seated as before, except that his arms should be resting easily on the working surface of a table or his desk. The elbows should be bent and the back, shoulders, head, hips and legs relaxed with just enough tonus to maintain a relaxed seated posture.
2. Present a visual-motor task that is within the child's motoric perceptual and conceptual abilities. Many of the tasks listed under language arts, writing and math in Readiness I would be appropriate for the child performing at the pre-school level. For the child who is

in a regular classroom and performing within his academic range but whose writing has been inadequate due to lack of movement development the following tasks may be used.

a. Scribbling

Give the child a crayon and a large sheet of paper. Ask him to scribble randomly on the paper while observing what he is doing. The goal is the maintenance of a relaxed position while using a writing tool without demands on the nature of the movement or its results. Observe carefully to see that no excess tension develops. Check feet and legs frequently; he may have them hooked around the legs of the chair, tied together, or positioned rigidly. You may see an unusually great amount of shuffling and shifting of position. Watch his neck and shoulders to see that excessive tension does not develop or that an atypical posture is not assumed in an attempt to relieve the tension.

(1) If tension develops, manipulate the involved muscle groups until relaxation is restored. Then continue the task.

(2) If an atypical posture develops, stop and restore the desired posture, then continue. Encourage the child to recognize when relaxation has been lost and the effect of this loss on his performance.

b. Increase the demand for perceptual control.

(1) Ask the child to trace a simple motif that has been drawn on a large sheet of paper with a marking pencil or crayon. Examples:

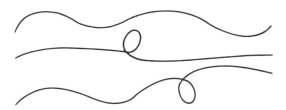

This line requires perceptual monitoring during the tracing, but because it is so broad and heavy, does not require precision of monitoring. Be sure that the motif extends across the midline of the child's body so that any development of tension at the midline can be detected. It should not, however, be more than 6 or 8 inches wider than the child's shoulders. Watch especially for tension in the neck and face during the task due to a breakdown in visual control or because the child is using his eyes to direct his hand rather than to monitor it.

If at this point, performance breaks down or the child cannot relax while performing, determine why. First, the child's fingers, hand, wrist, and arm may not be differentiated and coordinated to the degree necessary for the manipulation of a writing tool. If so, continue to work in those areas using specific movements, finger plays, and a variety of manipulative materials and tools.

Second, visual control may still be inadequate and the child therefore depends on body tension to help him align, move or control his eyes. If this is the case, more work must be done on visual differentiation, control and the visual to motor match.

Third, the child may be able to use his eyes and his hand and arm adequately but the demands of a complex perceptual motor task panic him and he reverts to an old habit learned before he developed kinesthetic awareness; that is, he uses his eyes to direct his hand rather than to monitor it. If so, introduce the tasks suggested under "Learning to Monitor" which follow.

LEARNING TO MONITOR THE HAND WITH THE EYES

Children who in the process of growing up do not develop adequate kinesthetic figure-ground and awareness often use their eyes to direct their movements rather than to monitor them. Even after kinesthetic awareness and automation is achieved through relaxation, such a child often reverts to the old habit of relying on his eyes rather than the newly developed kinesthesia when he is presented with a difficult perceptual-motor task. As a rule it is easy to detect the child whose eyes are directing his hand for his eyes are either locked onto his hand or precede it slightly as he plays, works, draws, writes and so on. At times his head and eyes will move in the direction the hand is to go, and usually the head (and eyes) moves closer and closer to the task.

The following activities are presented as a means of emphasizing attention to kinesthetic information from the hand and arm and encouraging the child to use his eyes to monitor rather than direct or control.

When working with very young children much tactual-kinesthetic exploration without vision should be encouraged.

For the four-, five- and six-year-olds, tactual-kinesthetic exploration and using templates, a raised tack, and enlarged Frostig alleys can be used. The older child should begin with tactual-kinesthetic exploration and work through subsequent stages.

USING TEMPLATES

1. The child should sit at a table with his shoulders, arms, legs and neck relaxed. Blindfold him, then present a simple template:

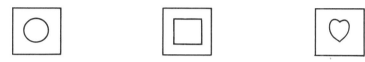

   Place his hand on the inside edge and ask him to slowly trace around it with his finger or fingers several times.
2. While he is still blindfolded, remove the template and place in front of him a paper covered with finger paint, very soft clay or any other media on which he can leave a trace with his finger; then ask the child to draw what he felt when tracing the template. If the design is adequate go to activity #3; if not, return to #1 and repeat until it is adequate.
3. While the child is still blindfolded, erase the pattern by smoothing out the media used, then remove the blindfold. Next the child is asked to draw the design again, repeating it until he is asked to stop. But before he starts the teacher tells him she is going to place her hands over his eyes or place a piece of cardboard between his eyes and the paper and that she will remove the cover from time to time. When she does his eyes should be on his hand and should follow it until the cover is replaced.

   The movement of the child's hand should not hesitate when the cover is removed or when it is replaced.

USING A RAISED TRACK

1. Make a track of a piece of wood approximately two inches wide. The length should be four to six inches wider than the child's shoulders. Other tracks may be made of sandpaper, tape, rope, etc. Place the track in front of the child on the table at a distance he can reach easily with his arms slightly bent. If necessary, hold it in place.
2. Cover his eyes with your hands or pass a piece of cardboard between his eyes and the task.

a. He then moves an object slowly along the track with both hands. The object may be anything that has weight and which can be held between his two hands. For example, a tape dispenser, a water faucet, a can of soup, etc.

b. On top of the object, tape a visual target made out of a one-inch square of paper with lines, randomly spaced, drawn on it with a narrow point felt tipped pen.

3. Instruct the child to move the object back and forth. Tell him that when your hands are removed he is to find the target with his eyes and watch it move.

a. He is not to hesitate when the hands are removed, but to keep moving the target. (Hands make the best blindfold as cloth or other material give a warning when it is being removed, whereas hands can be used to cover and uncover the eyes very rapidly).

4. The child is to watch the target all of the time. Be sure that his eyes do not precede the target. If they do, cover his eyes and begin again. Uncover the eyes at different places during the movement of the target so he will not learn to anticipate where to look; instead the eyes should be moving along under the cover in rhythm with the hands. First, he uses both hands together, back and forth from left to right. When the eyes and hands move smoothly together, he may use each hand separately. Finally, he may use his dominant hand and start his movement at his opposite side. During all of the activities above, the child is not to move his trunk or head, only his arms and his eyes.

USING ENLARGED FROSTIG ALLEYS

1. Introduce a simple alley and have the child move an object such as a block within the lines. The alleys should be broad and should extend two or three inches beyond the child's shoulders. Example:

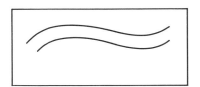

2. Have the child perform:

   a. As you interrupt vision.
   b. As his eyes continually monitor his hands.
      (If the child's hands tighten or there is tension in neck and face
      or if the head draws down toward the task it is a sign that the
      child is reverting to the old habit of depending on his eyes to
      direct his hands.)

3. Introduce additional alleys in which you gradually decrease the
   width and increase the complexity and finally do both.

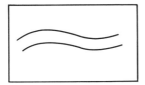 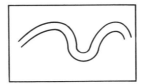 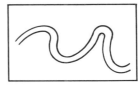

TRACING

1. Have the child trace motifs and simple letters:

   a. Using the cardboard to interrupt vision.
   b. With the eyes continuously monitoring the hand, watch for ten-
      sion that may indicate the child has reverted to the old habit of a
      reversed match, i.e. his eyes are leading his hand. When the child
      can perform adequately and without tension, continue with
      copying, as described below.

COPYING

   Place a clean sheet of paper on the child's desk. Draw a motif
across the top of the sheet. This motif should be sufficiently complex
to demand perceptual control and a certain amount of concentration.
It should extend across the midline of the child's body. Ask the child to
copy this motif. Leave the original copy in sight so that this is a copying task not a visual memory task.
   At this point another problem may be detected. The child's eyes
may follow along the presented pattern ignoring his hand and its performance. We call this remote tracing. The hand is simply following
the motion of the eyes. What we want the child to do is look at the presented pattern, translate it from a visual pattern into a kinesthetic one
and then reproduce it kinesthetically using the eyes to monitor. To get

a proper performance you may have to show the pattern to the child, then cover it and have him reproduce from memory. For the older child who is reading and whose academic requirements include copying from printed material, expand the copying tasks by presenting:

1. Repetitious letters   *aaa lll mmm*
2. Combination of letters   *elelel mnmn wewew*
3. Words
4. Sentences
5. Simple printed material

Gradually increase the complexity of the printed material until the child is copying at his reading level.

chapter 8

Preparation for Language Arts

By now, the child should have had much time to experiment with babbling and jargon which has helped to differentiate his throat muscles, larynx muscles, tongue, jaw and lips, thus associating sounds and muscle movement.

He should have experienced hours of associating sounds with postural movements.

He has learned to use vocalizations for pleasure as well as communication. Ecolalia is prevalent. He is now ready to learn language. He is physically and mentally ready to associate the name with the object and to make the grand discovery that everything has a name.

The child needs to further develop his feedback system—i.e., his ability to monitor sounds and words in relation to his behavior.

As he gains more control of his movements in space and time, he will begin to add adjectives and adverbs to describe the many more objects he is encountering and the many more movements he is discovering within himself and between himself and others and between himself and objects. As his movements become more diversified his perceptions and language become more specific. He begins to express himself as he moves, to move, then express what he has done, and later will state what he is going to do and then do it. He uses "what" and "where" and "why" statements to verify motor and motor-perceptual data.

Gestures and jargon drop off as the child elaborates his use of language; i.e., naming, identifying, stating function, stating action, use of plurals and experimentation with language in a nonsensical or fanciful manner.

The child with learning disabilities may need help in one, several or all of the areas listed. Remember that movements must come naturally and easily before the child can give his attention to speech and that tension can interfere with language, both receptive and expressive. If there are signs of movement difficulties, gross or fine, or signs of tension, work to eliminate these before you work for speech and language (see previous stages for suggestions). Remember this is also true of children working at higher levels.

SOUNDS

ENJOYMENT OF SOUND

Continue to encourage the child to use sounds and words for pleasure as well as communication—the pleasure of movement, the pleasure of sound and the pleasure of rhythm. (The normal child performing at this level is particularly fond of rhythmic use of language and uses it in many ways). A key word in an adult's request or conversation may catch his fancy and he will make a little repetitious rhyme of it. Or he will pick an adult's or other child's expression and repeat it rhythmically. Later he may use rhyming words or sounds instead of simply repeating the same word; thus, "laddie" might elicit something like "daddy," or "paddie." "Body" would elicit something like "lodie" or "doddy." He may even make requests or comments or retell a simple experience in sing-song fashion, often repeating all or part.

Do not discourage this rhythmic play on words even though it may sound foolish coming from the older child. In fact, it may be necessary to encourage it.

SOUND COMBINED WITH MOVEMENT

1. Encourage vigorous sound with very active movements.
2. When moving slowly or doing a quiet task, the vocalization should be mild and quiet—crooning, murmuring, chanting.
3. Say what the child is doing as he does it and encourage him to say it also; for example, *up, down, open the door, in the basket,* and so on.
4. When his movements are rhythmic, try to get simultaneous rhythmic vocalization. It can be as simple as placing a block from one box to another as he says, "another, another, another," or chanting, "round and round and round" while he rides on the merry-go-round.
5. If the vocalizations are rhythmic, introduce simultaneous rhythmic movements.

6. Permit him to talk aloud as he works and plays. If the child has never done so, he should be encouraged to talk as he performs. The child uses this procedure to maintain and solidify his perceptions. He is communicating with himself, thus matching what he sees and hears to what he is doing. He is labeling his percepts.

VOCABULARY

The child's vocabulary may be small and made up of single words and stock phrases which he uses for pleasure, often inadequately. The inadequacy does not bother the child unless someone finds fault with it. (There are always exceptions to these statements.)

One child may add words without any noticeable effort and does not attempt to say that which he has no words to express. Another child may question or stutter as he endeavors to go beyond immediate abilities. Still another spends months practicing new words and the combination of old words in new or varied ways. Such a child may show real joy when a phrase is mastered and may repeat it often.

Some children voluntarily echo almost everything they hear. If this behavior continues too long it interferes with spontaneous language.

ATTACHING NAMES TO OBJECTS AND
PICTURES OF OBJECTS AND ACTIONS

1. Use every means available to help each child increase his vocabulary. Don't teach words for the sake of learning words. Make sure that each word is meaningful to the child. Give him the opportunity to experience and explore the object or action that his nouns and verbs represent
2. Use objects, actions and pictures from the following classifications:
   a. Self: body parts; clothing; food; actions.
   b. Home and immediate environment: family members; household articles; animals (pets); sounds; neighbors; weather elements— snow, rain, wind, etc.; yard; grocery store.
   c. Classroom: classmates and teachers; familiar classroom objects; sounds; actions of others.

ACTIVITIES

1. Naming of objects and people: Continue identification and naming of new objects, people, pictures and animals.

2. Relating the picture to the object (beginning preparation for later use of words and numbers to represent objects):

   a. Present tasks that require the child to find the picture that matches the object and reverse.
   b. Have the child match a group of pictures with a group of objects and vice versa.
   c. Talk about the names of the objects and pictures when working with the child.

3. Relating picture to picture:

   a. Present a picture and have the child match it to one of several pictures (Picture Lotto Games).
   b. Present the child with two groups of pictures and have him find the matched pairs. Begin with small groups, two or three of each.
      (1) Arrange one group in front of him. Present the other group of pictures in a pile or as a deck of cards.
      (2) Present two piles of pictures for him to sort into pairs.
      (3) Present all pictures in one pile to be sorted.

4. Auditory recognition:

   a. Have the child locate a named picture, using picture cards.
   b. Present several pictures, name one, have the child choose the one named.
   c. Use a variety of picture books that have several clear pictures on each page.
   d. Make scrap books of newly learned pictures and use for reviewing names.

5. Naming (picture cards, picture books and scrap books):

   a. Point to the pictures one at a time and have the child name each.
   b. Use picture books with several pictures on a page. Ask the child to point to and name each of the pictures.
   c. Use group pictures that show a variety of objects, people and animals. Ask the child to find, point to and name as many as he can.

6. Identification and naming of actions:

   a. Move among the children as they work or play and call attention to the action that each is performing. Examples:
      Mary is jumping.
      John is sitting.
      John is scribbling.
   b. Have the child perform an action which he hears in a story or sees in a picture.

    c. Have the child match paired action pictures.

    d́. Have him find the picture that denotes what he sees another doing.

    e. Have the child close his eyes and listen as another person moves, then ask him to choose the picture that show the correct action. Example: bouncing a ball; clapping; singing; jumping; pounding.

    f. Have the child perform a named activity. For example, the teacher would tell the child to lie on his stomach, stand, sit, jump, run, clap, etc.

    g. Have the child name the action.

        (1) Listen to performing person and name.

        (2) Look at performer and name.

        (3) Look, point and name action in pictures.

        (When working with action words (verbs), remember that at first the child may use the root verb regardless of person, number or subject. There may be few if any tense distinctions. As he learns to add "ing" or "ed" to verbs he may use them indiscriminately for awhile.)

VISUAL SEARCH

1. Before a child can easily and adequately perform a task that requires him to choose one object or picture out of several he must be able to search. He must move his eyes from one picture to another without missing any of them. If the child cannot control his eyes adequately to scan the material presented, go back to the activities for developing eye control and visual motor match.

2. Tasks of identification and naming can be continued if the person working with the child points to each of the things to be identified; encourage the child to point to each. If motor control is so poor that he skips over some of the pictures, direct his hand for him and work on previous suggestions for movement control.

MOVEMENT CONTROL

1. The child who is too bilateral or undifferentiated may point or grasp with both hands at the same time, because he cannot move one without involving the other. It won't interfere if he points to or picks up the same picture with the two hands. Such a child needs help to differentiate the two sides of his body until he can point, reach, grasp and release with each hand without moving or tensing the opposite hand.

2. For those children who crumble, crush and tear the learning materials use sturdy cardboard backing and spray with plastic. Work diligently for movement control.

SPACE AND TIME

1. All of the preceding activities can and should be extended into space to encourage memory over time and to make sure that gross movement does not interfere with memory. If it does, more work may be needed in differentiation, balance, coordination and locomotion.

    a. Place a group of pictures across the room. Then ask the child to get a picture like the one you are showing or the one you have named.
    b. Vary the child's starting position (on floor or stomach, seated on floor, seated at desk, etc.)

COMMUNICATION

At this stage the teacher should not be too concerned with perfect pronunciation or proper use of words. The important thing is verbal communication. If the child can make others understand what he is trying to convey, then he has communicated. Verbal confusions are common and often a source of amusement to adults. For example, if the child says "shirt is broken" for a hole in his shirt, "its my ready," for my turn or "I tongued it" (when licking an ice cream cone) instead of "I licked it," he can be readily understood. Do not laugh and tell him that he said it wrong and should have said it another way. Give him the correct words in your answer. For example, "Yes, your shirt does have a hole in it." "Yes, I see the hole in your shirt." The accent is on the word "hole."

At this level the child is living in two worlds and uses a dual system of verbal relationships. In one system he uses his own private symbols to interpret his interactions with the concrete into symbolic language. The second system involves his verbal interactions with other persons. His questions are endless as he seeks verification of his own symbolizations. Therefore, the answers given to his what's, who's and why's should help him correct his private interpretations and move him toward the agreed upon relationships between verbal signs and their referents rather than stress additional information. He in turn uses and applies the new terms to his own actions before he is secure in using them for communication. He monitors his verbalizations through his dramatizations.

WORDS

If the child is still dependent on gestures for most of his communications, encourage him to use words to make his needs and desires known and to express himself. Give him time. Do not speak for him. Accept initial sounds, simple words or descriptive words, such as "d" for drink, "milk" for drink, "to drink from" when he wants a glass, "get" for "I will get it." Pay attention to whatever means he uses to make known his desires for an explanation of new sights, sounds or experiences.

If the child continues to have difficulty with naming or use of words, recheck to see if he has the necessary relaxation and differentiation of jaw, tongue and lips. Watch to see if he is attending visually as you say the word, and make sure that he is attending auditorily. The visual-auditory match is essential to the learning of first words.

If the child can differentiate the parts of his mouth and attend visually and auditorily but still has difficulty, the motor kinesthetic approach outlined by Young and Hawk[1] may be helpful.

PHRASES

As soon as the child can use words, encourage the use of phrases. Introduce adjectives, prepositions and pronouns that apply to the child and his actions. Example: hot, cold, wet, pretty, up high, down, in my, mine. Make sure that the child has experienced each. To teach the word, introduce it during a related experience. If the child can speak in phrases and sentences, but doesn't do it unless it is absolutely necessary or if it all seems to roll out in one breath, it would indicate holding of breath due to tension in stomach, chest and neck. If so, work for relaxation first, then speech, keeping the child relaxed as he verbalizes (see relaxation recommendations in previous stages).

LEARNING TO EXPRESS HIMSELF

1. As soon as the child can use words and phrases, encourage him to talk about objects, actions and events. Keep in mind that to him there may be only the immediate environment. Don't expect long histories, deep meanings or far-reaching implications, only a brief description of the visible here and now.
2. Encourage the child to ask what, who and where. If adults in his life always rush in to supply the child's needs or the name of each object, the child will not learn to ask. He will have no need to ask. When answering, use words he can understand and be brief. Keep in mind that he is asking for the name of the object, its placement in his en-

---

[1]E. Young and S. Hawks, *Motor Kinesthetic Speech Training* (Palo Alto, California: Stanford University Press, 1938).

vironment, or for verification of his own interpretation.

3. Once the child is aware of "what" and "who," encourage him to find cause and effect of movements, actions, events. That is, the child should learn not only to say what is happening, but also "who" or "what" caused it to happen. Accept one word, a phrase, or a simple sentence as an answer. Asking for an elaboration may cause the child to lose the thought pattern. (At first the child must observe what is happening).

4. When phrases and short sentences come easily, he should also be able to:

    a. Make simple comparisons and use the words "too," meaning also, and "like," meaning same.

    b. Be aware and express that objects and people have points in common, such as "I don't cry; babies cry," or "I don't shave; daddies shave."

    c. Make occasional conditional statements. Example: "It will burn if I touch"; "I will stay inside if it rains."

    d. Verbalize his actions in order or sequence. Example: "I get drink then I color"; "Go outside, after eat lunch, and Johnny do it, afterwhile."

5. The courtesy words "please" and "thank you" should be encouraged, but not forced. Too often adults require a child to say "thank you" when he is not thankful. In fact, he may even feel resentful. Remember it is better to make direct demands of children performing at this level. Decisions are difficult for them and "please" denotes a choice. "Do it to please me or don't do it." The child may not want to please you at the moment and therefore have every right to refuse.

CLASSIFICATIONS

As the child acquires names for a variety of objects, actions and events, he begins to develop the idea of general class. The process is slow and distortions are often seen. In the beginning there may be a complete absence of either individual identity or general class. For example, a change of clothes changes the person. A complex object depends on one of its elements which is seen as representing the whole; thus a dog may be an animal, but at the same time all animals may be dogs. Many different black cars may be the same car re-appearing. Then come the specific words for each specific object within a familiar class. Example: family—daddy, Joe, boy, man. Animals—dog, cat, bird.

Finally the child begins to generalize and he applies general meaning to general classes; for example, family, pets, food and specific meaning to specific classes, that is, blocks, dogs, balls, babies and so on.

DEVELOPMENT OF CONCEPT OF CLASSIFICATION

1. Introduce and talk about objects and pictures of objects that belong to a class. Talk about the class name as well as the names of the things that belong to it.
2. Present tasks that require the child to choose objects or pictures that belong to a general or specific class.

   Examples: Finding the things we eat or wear.

   Finding the things that one can play with or sit on.

   Finding people, animals.

   Finding the balls, blocks, babies, dogs.
3. Sorting and Grouping.

   a. Present tasks that require the child to sort and group.

   b. The child must now keep two or more classes in mind as he sorts a number of objects or pictures into their respective groups.

COMBINING WORDS INTO SENTENCES

The child's first sentences will be brief, incomplete and repetitious. They may be any of the following combinations:

> subject—verb
> subject and modifying adjective
> subject and adverb of place
> verb and object
> question word with noun or verb

The child's word order may vary; he may omit the verb or the subject of the sentence or conjunctions. The preposition is the one single part of speech most commonly omitted.

At first he combines two words then three, four and five and so on as he progresses through Stage I. Thus if he said, "Boy ride" in the beginning, he should be saying, "That boy is riding his bike," or something similar when he enters the next stage.

PRONOUNCING WORDS SO
OTHERS CAN UNDERSTAND

Pronunciation improves very slowly during this stage. Pronunciation should be stressed *only* if the child's verbalization is not intelligible to others. Even then, tongue, jaw and lip movements should be emphasized before pronunciation. As the movements are learned and elaborated, pronunciation may improve without any specific effort in that direction. There are a few common distortions, such as the vowel distortions: ah want—I want, bee-bee—baby, mulk—milk.

Consonant distortions are more universal and early sentences can often be understood only because they are accompanied by appropriate actions. Common consonant substitutions are:

> w for r—woom for room
> t for c—tat for cat
> d for g—all done for all gone
> d for j—dump for jump

Less common:

> w for l—wook for look
> b for v—begtable for vegetable

Double consonants often replaced by single ones:

> d or f for th
> f for sh

The consonants may be split and only one used:

> floor becomes foor
> clean becomes cean
> cry becomes cy
> broke becomes boke
> spoon becomes poon
> stone becomes tone
> splash becomes plash

The child may also soften or omit final consonant sounds—han for hand, or the whole first or final syllable:

> mato for tomato
> cause for because
> op for open

PREPARATION FOR WRITING

The activities of the past stage prepared the child for the day when he could pick up a writing tool and make a mark. To prepare himself to make marks and scribbles, every child must spend many months practicing the same type of movements without a writing tool, as he differentiates his arms and hands and moves toys about in the air and across various surfaces.

In the earliest stages of scribbling, eye-hand coordination is not required, only pre-learned movements. Soon, however, the child begins to attend visually to the trace that he leaves when scribbling. At first he attends after the trace has been made; later, at the time that he is making it. Unless the second stage occurs, he will not be able to structure and combine his scribbles into art and mathematical or language symbols.

MOVEMENT AND MANIPULATION OF OBJECTS IN PREPARATION FOR WRITING.

1. Clay Play

    a. Encourage the child to pound, pinch, poke, squeeze and roll the clay. Poking can be done with each finger and thumb and later with a variety of tools.
    b. After he pinches off a variety of pieces he can re-combine the pieces—his first creation of form made up of parts.

2. Sand and mud

    a. Have the child use his hands, fingers, arms and feet to mark, write, scribble in the sand.
    b. Encourage him to shape damp sand or earth into various free form shapes, make mud pies, roads and so on.
    c. Have him walk in the sand, cover parts of his body with it, use his feet and toes to make prints and marks.

3. Finger paints

    a. Hand movements—do with both hands simultaneously and each individually.
        (1) Use whole hand, flat and relaxed. Push paint around.
        (2) Make a fist, thumb up. Pound here and there.
        (3) Use side of hand (little finger side), fingers held straight. Make lines this way and that.
        (4) Try finger tips. Make them squirm through paint.
        (5) Scratch with fingernails, lightly and softly.

(6) Use one finger or thumb.
(7) Use thumb and one finger, then two fingers, then three fingers; now all fingers. Vary the fingers (thumb, index and little finger, thumb, second fingers and third, thumb, second and little finger, etc.)
(8) Hold fingers stiff and paint with whole palmar surface of fingers. Then paint with whole surface of each finger separately.
(9) Make a fist, using knuckles; rotate lightly and softly.
(10) Bend just the fingers and paint with the finger joints.
(11) Use the back of the whole hand.
  b. To increase wrist flexibility and range of motion:
(1) Stabilize forearm and put little finger side of hand on paper. Slide the hand with fingers together to the back and to the front. This action may be done singularly or with both hands together.
(2) Stabilize forearm and put palm surfaces of hand on paper. Slide hand with fingers held together to the right and to the left. May be done with both hands together or singularly.
(3) Make a dot on the paper. Place the child's thumb on the dot. Make a circle of dots around the center thumb dot. Have the child move his index finger from one outside dot to another. This increases wrist rotation. Vary the outside dot positions closer or farther from thumb and require wider sweeps around the circle with the finger. Change fingers. May be done singularly and with both hands together.
  c. Using the arm
(1) Paint with the surface of the forearm using wide sweeps of the arm; dab and pound.
(2) Use the elbow—dab, make circles, curves, lines.
(3) Use the wrist, front and back, to dab, scribble and draw.
  d. Make prints with finger paints.
(1) Finger prints.
(2) Hand prints.
(3) Foot prints.
4. Puppets—encourage play with finger and hand puppets.
5. Snap clothes pins—have the child place them on the edge of a box or can or on a rope line.
6. Page turning:
  a. Have the child do smooth rhythmic turning of pages one at a time.

      b. Have him turn the pages from right to left with his right hand and left to right with his left.

      c. If he has difficulty begin with books that have thick pages.

      d. The easiest method is to grasp the page at the top near the outside corner.

7. Levers, slides, dials and knobs.

      a. Present opportunities for the child to move levers, slides, dials and so on in vertical, horizontal and circular directions. These actions should cause something to happen such as a door open, music play and so on if you wish to teach causality as well as coordination.

8. Drum, pound, and tap. Supply a variety of opportunities for:

      a. Pounding:
         (1) With fist.
         (2) With hammer.
         (3) With other things.

      b. Drumming on drums, tin cans, boxes, tom-tom, etc. With hands, fingers, fists, sticks, etc.

      c. Tapping on the table top, tambourine, keyboard, etc.

9. Pet, rub and scrub. Emphasize the difference in pressure when doing each. Use such words as easy, slow and gentle when petting. To pet gently the child needs good movement control.

MARKING

Earliest markings are jabs and dashes. The writing tool is usually held in a palmar grasp. If an older child holds his writing tool in this manner but is writing or if he holds it more correctly but very tightly and rigidly, put the writing tool in a piece of clay. Have the child grasp and squeeze until the natural imprint of his fingers are in the clay; then encourage a relaxed grasp as he marks on the board or paper. In the meantime help him relax his arms, neck and shoulders and teach him how to work relaxed. Wrist differentiation may also be necessary. As the child learns to hold the adapted writing tool, gradually decrease the size of the clay holder and re-shape it so that it follows more closely the lines of the tool.

Give the child a large crayon or broad piece of chalk and ask him to make marks on the chalkboard or a piece of paper. (If poor balance interferes in any way, if the child holds onto the board, can't stand still, uses wide stance, etc., have the child perform seated and anchor him in the chair with a seat belt, if necessary). Whenever possible the chalkboard should stand free of the wall so that the child's legs are under the board while seated. If these adjustments need to be made, stress relaxation and/or balance activities until the child can maintain balance while working when seated and standing.

SCRIBBLING

If the child is beyond the marking stage, ask him to scribble. If he does not understand the command or if he uses only finger or wrist movements, demonstrate. Use full arm movements that result in large slow flowing scribbles on the chalkboard or paper.

Scribbling should be continued throughout this stage. The normal child spends months scribbling before perceivable form begins to emerge. The child's scribbles should be continuous and repetitious and include circular, vertical, horizontal, diagonal and alternating lines. If you do not see all of the preceding, do not teach the child how to make them; rather, check to see if he has the necessary arm movements. If not, help him develop the needed differentiation.

1. Vary his scribbiing. Encourage him to use each hand; both hands simultaneously; both hands on the same writing tool.
2. Vary the tool used for scribbling—chalk, crayon, felt pen, paint brush. Permit and encourage the child to make scribble pictures using two or more colors.
3. Vary the child's working surface:

   a. Smooth and rough.
   b. Large sheets of paper and chalkboard to encourage large free flowing scribbles.
   c. Small sheets of paper (8 ½ x 11) or marked off space on the board to call the child's attention to the background area and to encourage placement of the scribbles in relation to the background.

4. Have him scribble to music. Vary tempo and melodies.

PLACING AND LEAVING A MARK

1. As soon as the child attends visually to what his hand creates, simple placement tasks can be assigned. (Remember, however, to continue to allow plenty of free scribble, drawing, and painting time.)

   a. Have the child place his finger on a small object or mark.
   b. Have him place an object on another object or mark (at this stage we are not asking for matching, only placement).
   c. Introduce simple collage. Prepare the child's paper:

(1) With an area of colored glue in which he can place a variety of *found* objects.

(2) By placing colored glue at various points and asking him to place his object in the glue.

d. Placing to leave a print.

(1) Imprinting in clay: Have the child find and use interesting objects that when pressed into a slab of clay will leave varied imprints. Example: spool, curler, spoon, small spring, end of pencil, button.

(2) Print making

(a) Use a variety of *found* objects that can be pressed against an ink pad and then upon a sheet of paper to leave a mark.

(b) He is to print on a given spot or spots that are marked. (Montgomery, Chandler. *Art for Teachers of Children.*, 2d. ed. Columbus, Ohio: Charles E. Merrill Publishing Company, 1973)

e. Placing a dot in a given place.

To perform the tasks that require placement or marking in a given spot the child must be able to hold his eyes on the spot as his hand moves in, and his arm must have enough control to place the object or the point of the writing tool on the correct spot. When he first uses the writing tool his dot may have a tail

or be a short line. Example. ✎ ✎   If he misses the spot repeatedly his visual-motor development should be re-analyzed, particularly his ability to hold a fixation and his reach, grasp and release.

(1) Feed the bird or birds.

(2) Put a center in the flower or flowers.

IMITATING A LINE

To imitate a drawn line the child does not copy the line but rather imitates movements from the top of the paper to the bottom or from one side to the other. He translates his eye movements from up to down or side to side into a corresponding arm movement. Again we must realize that the child first had to learn the arm movements and that his eyes became aware of an up and down or side to side movement through the watching of self movements. Otherwise the visual to motor translation could not be made.

The following steps precede the imitation of a drawn line.

1. Arm and hand movements through space.
2. Eye movements.
3. Visual attention to arm and hand movements.
4. Visual attention to the movement of objects through space.
5. Imitation of the arm and hand movement of another person.
6. Imitation of the movement of an object (the move unseen).
7. Imitation of the drawing of a line, vertical or horizontal.

The adult draws a long line down or across paper or chalkboard. Make sure that you have the child's attention throughout the drawing; then ask the child to make one like it. The child's first lines will not be straight and direct but will meander along in the proper direction. Example:

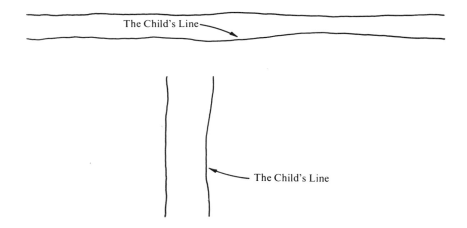

8. Copying of a vertical and horizontal line.

CIRCLES

1. Imitating circular motion.
2. Noting that it is a closed circle stopping short, then adding closure.
3. Copying.

ABOVE AND BELOW RELATIONSHIP (COPYING)

1. Present the child with a picture of an apple (or other fruit) without a stem, then show him another picture of an apple with the stem accented. Example: Point out that your apple has a stem but his does not, point to it, make sure that he knows what the stem is, then have him draw a stem on his apple.

    a. Present a variety of different pictures, fruits and other objects familiar to the child. Example: yo-yo, balloon on a string, etc.
    b. When the child can do them individually ask for stems on a row of apples or scattered ones.
    c. Finally ask him to copy the whole apple, singly and in a series.

2. Same as No. 1 except that you present objects that require the child to attach a line below the object and follow the steps listed above. Example: balloon on a string, stick on a lollipop, string on a kite, stem on a flower, etc.

PREPARATION FOR MATH

COMPARING AND RELATING WHOLE OBJECTS

1. Single piece inlay puzzles.

    The child is to match and fit the form to the cutout area. Use simple three-to six-piece puzzles. (Include many of the classifications listed at the beginning of the unit on language arts.) Examples:

    a. Make sure the child is looking as he works. Do not permit him to "fumble" the form into place. If vision or eye control is poor, have the child examine the object and the cut out area tactually to find the correct match.
    b. Another time have him indicate where each piece goes and then place the form.
    c. Point to a "cut out" and have him find the matching form.

2. Introduction to Gross Differences.

    a. Give the child opportunities to explore and experiment.
       (1) Big and little or large and small.
       (2) Hot and cold.

(3) Loud and quiet.
(4) Heavy and light.
  (a) Begin with extreme differences.
  (b) Help the child use visual, tactual-kinesthetic and auditory means of exploration.

b. When presented with big and little or long and short blocks, the child should be able to learn to copy a row of big ones, long ones, short ones or little ones. However, he may not be able to choose a big or little one when asked. At this time he is developing an awareness of sameness rather than differences.

EXPLORATION OF THE PARTS OF FORMS

1. Location and identification.

   a. Have the child:
      (1) Imitate another person as he moves one or more parts.
      (2) Locate and identify when named: parts of self, others, animals and objects.
      (3) Name and locate or locate and name parts.
      (4) Match pictures of parts, such as finding all the pictures of legs, eyes, wheels and so on.

   b. Find missing parts and recognize altered parts on people.
      (1) Have a person come into the room with one object of clothing missing, changed about or distorted. The child observes what is absent or different and then arranges himself like the example.
      (2) A person acting as a model changes position while the child's eyes are covered. The child looks, imitates and then names the change.

   c. Have the child find gross incongruities in pictures. Example: Person without a head, car without wheels and so on.

2. Manipulation and combination of parts by the child. Have the child:

   a. Add two, three or four parts to a person, animal or object puzzle.
   b. Work two-and three-piece puzzles that require attention to the whole as well as the parts. Example:

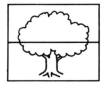   Nongeometric Animals, People, Vehicles, etc.

    c. Play with and solve two- to four-piece, "take apart-put together" toys and insert puzzles.

    d. Manipulate, explore and work with a variety of peg boards.

       (1) Peg boards:

          (a) One size of holes and peg.

          (b) Two sizes of holes and pegs.

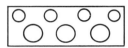 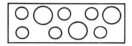

       (2) Insert boards that have several different types of objects, several objects in a category, and gradation of size. Example:

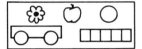  

       (3) Nesting toys (see Stack and Build under "Visual-Motor Match" in this section).

       (4) Stacking toys.

    e. Work with large piece construction sets such as Lego (2"x4" blocks) Connector, Artiplay and large Tinker toys.

    f. String beads to make bracelets, necklaces, ropes.

    g. Snip with scissors.

       (1) Give the child ropes of clay, dough or strips of other resistive material that snips easily. At first he may need to use both hands on the scissors. Later he will be able to snip with one hand but may not yet be able to hold the material in the other hand. He will probably place it on the table to cut.

    h. Play with gadget boxes that are made up of locks, hooks, snaps, slide bolts and other objects that fit together.

LOCATION OF OBJECTS IN SPACE

1. In a large area

    a. Have the child locate objects in each room in the house; in the yard; in the classroom.

    b. Have the child locate all sections of a room as you name them—window, door, curtain, wall, floor, ceiling—make sure he knows whole areas, not just spots. Use a doll house to convey idea of the whole wall, whole floor, etc.

    c. Categorize furniture, actions, etc. according to the room with which they are associated.

        (1) Where is the refrigerator? (In what room?) Where is your bed?

        (2) Where do we eat? Where do you take your bath?

        (3) Sort furniture and put into the correct rooms in a doll house.

    d. Have the child name the objects as you point to them.

    e. The child names and then locates.

    f. The child locates an object, then names.

2. In a small area: Procedure is the same as in location of objects in a large area except that the child now locates smaller spaces such as table or desk top, and finer visual and visual-motor control is required.

EXPLORATION OF SPACE

1. Terms to be experienced and learned: here, on, off, up, down, into, out of and under.

2. Relationships to be learned:

    a. Body parts to self. Example: Touch your nose with your tongue. Put your hand on your foot. Put your toe on your nose. Put your hands under you.

    b. Self to objects. Example: Get on the box. Climb down. Get under your desk. Go outside.

3. Sequence to be used.

    a. In Imitation:

        (1) Child imitates actions of another.

        (2) Child imitates and says what he is doing.

    b. From verbal commands:

        (1) Teacher gives commands, child performs.

        (2) One child gives command, another performs.

    c. Verbalize and perform:

        (1) Child says and does simultaneously.

        (2) Teacher questions the child about his performance. Example: Where is your arm? Where are you? What did you do with your toe?

4. Variations. To insure the building of concepts, rather than a few memorized acts, vary every aspect of the task.

   a. Vary the position of the child's body. He could be lying on his stomach, back, side, kneeling, sitting or standing.
   b. Have the child use single and combined parts of his body, as well as his whole body, i.e., one hand, both hands, one foot, his head, a hand and foot, etc.
   c. Vary the objects used.
   d. Vary the environment in which he performs, i.e., classroom, play yard, park, and so on.

5. Movement of the whole body (space and time).

   a. Present a combination of relationships and changes in body position. The obstacle courses suggested in the previous stage may be used. Add additional obstacles that require the child to step, walk and climb.
   b. Apply the terms and use the variations listed above.

6. Moving and manipulating objects through space and time. Supply the following and similar materials for manipulation, transportation and exploration:

   a. Small objects to be moved by hand into space and through space: stacking toys (vertical space); aligning or ordering toys (horizontal space); beads and string; peg boards; furnished doll houses and barns, etc.; puzzles; building blocks of various sizes (large and small); small trains, cars, trucks (movement through time and space); sand and water toys and places to use them; tea set (interactions between persons in time); house cleaning materials.
   b. Movement of large objects. Have the child lift and move blocks, chairs, stuffed toys, etc. Encourage quiet placement as well as movement to enhance development of movement control.
   c. Sequential handling of objects, large and small.
      (1) Have the child pick up and place in a container each item in a row of objects as they are named in order.
      (2) Have the child point to each object in a row of objects as they are named.
      (3) Have the child point to and name objects or pictures that have been placed in a horizontal or vertical row. He is to point to and name them in order.
   d. Use of objects that the child can ride.
      (1) Riding toy that does not require peddling but a push or pull of the legs upon the floor.

(2) Wagon.

(3) Peddle-type vehicle in which the child needs only to move forward with his legs alternately.

(4) Tricycle.

e. The child learns to ride 1, 3 and 4 above in the order listed and usually follows the learning sequence listed below:

(1) Plays with the parts of the vehicle—turn wheels, move handle, turn on light, etc.

(2) Pushes it about with his hands.

(3) Pulls the wagon, walks the kiddie car.

(4) Porpels properly.

(5) Uses to transport other objects.

Numbers 4 and 5 may not be achieved during this period of learning.

7. Organization of objects in space using arrangement of blocks.

a. The following presentations should be used.

(1) The child observes the building of a pattern, then makes one like it.

(2) A pattern is constructed behind a cover or screen, then uncovered and the child copies.

(3) A pattern is constructed behind a screen, shown to the child for several seconds, then re-covered. He then copies from memory.

b. Suggested materials—6 blocks 8 x 4 x 2 inches. (Later use 8 x 2 x 2 inch blocks.) Arrange three of the blocks and have the child copy the pattern using the other three blocks.

c. Suggested patterns:

(1) Horizontal patterns

(a) Flat

(b) On edge

(c) Upright

(2) Vertical patterns

(a) Stack flat

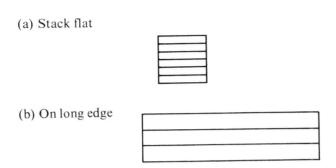

(b) On long edge

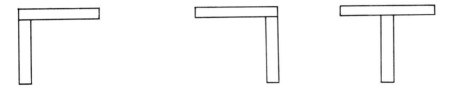

(3) Mid position and relationships. Use two of the blocks and build the following patterns. Have the child copy:

d. Presentation.

(1) The child watches as you arrange the blocks.
(2) The blocks are arranged behind a cover. The cover is then removed and the child copies.
(3) Begin as in "b" but replace the cover after the child takes a good look at the pattern, thus requiring him to copy from memory.

8. Location of actions in space and time.

a. Continue to stress "here" and "now," "start" and "stop."
b. Associate daily activities with day and night using activities and pictures. For example, relate play and sleep, getting up and going to bed, etc., with day and night or darkness and light or sun and moon.
c. Associate time with events that have already been established "after lunch we will paint," or "we will put our crayons away, then we will sing" and so on.
d. Associate the activities with today and tomorrow.

9. Propulsion and receipt of an object.
   a. Using a large ball to encourage bilateral arm coordination.
      (1) Position the child according to his ability to maintain balance or use all the following positions for variety: seated on the floor; cross legged, legs extended and open; seated in a chair or on a stool; standing.
      (2) Encourage the child to use the ball in a variety of ways, for example:
         (a) Bounce it to another person.
         (b) Catch it when bounced to him.
         (c) Bounce and catch the ball himself, against a wall, on the floor.
         (d) Toss to another person, both over-handed and under-handed.
         (e) Catch it when tossed to him.
   b. Using a small ball, bean bag or other suitable object, have the child.
      (1) Roll it: toward a goal, to another person, to knock down a group of objects, through an opening.
      (2) Toss it: into a container, through a hoop or other opening, to a person.

PREPARATION FOR READING

During this stage pre-reading activities continue. The child is involved in associations of things, people and processes. He learns and talks about the things he will read about later. Before we can teach a child to read he must be able to speak adequately (except in rare cases) and he must be able to communicate. Only then can we convey to him that reading is talking or communication written down.

There are, however, several specific types of activities that apply directly to the reading process. These can and should be introduced at this time.

EXPOSURE TO BOOKS AND READING

1. Let the child see adults and other children enjoying reading.
2. Supply opportunities for him to hear people reading aloud to themselves and others so that he will associate reading with talking.
3. Read from a variety of materials to the child (books, labels, signs, etc.).

   a. Use books with individual clear pictures that are closely associated with the printed material. At first the child may just look; a little later he can point to the pictures as the proper word is spoken and finally he will name the pictures. He finds excitement in the recognition of familiar things. Realistic and sharply defined pictures are best. Under each picture there should be one descriptive word or a single descriptive line. Example: boy, dog, dogs bark, the boy is running.
   b. Read simple stories about things the child has experienced or subjects of interest to the child. These should be very short. The child's attention span is no more than 2 or 3 minutes long. He will want to hear the same stories repeated many times in the same way each time.
   c. Occasionally read aloud from an adult book, newspaper, magazine, or book of poems as the children are resting or playing quietly. If the reading voice is pleasant, expressive and rhythmic, it can be as restful as music. If the material is read with enjoyment, the child will associate the joy with the act of reading and he will in turn enjoy the sound and rhythm of the voice whether he understands the words or not. Best of all, he will be a part of the "magic" of reading long before he can do it himself.

LEARNING TO LISTEN

1. If a child is too hyperactive to sit or lie quietly as you read, help him learn to relax, learn to remain quietly relaxed and to move parts of himself without overflow movement into other parts of his body.
2. When he can make fine differentiated movements without exploding into action but still needs to drain off excess motor energy in order to sit or lie still, permit him to have something in his hands that can be manipulated quietly as he rests and/or listens—i.e., a piece of clay, a string, a "worry stone", etc.

RHYTHM

Introduce activities that require simple rhythmic movements or sequential activities, for rhythm will play a major role in the child's ability to move his eyes back and forth across the printed page. Sequencing will be necessary for word recognition and the reading of words.

1. Non-movement *vs* movement.
   a. Encourage the child to relax and remain perfectly still for a period of time.

(1) Use a variety of positions. On the floor, on his back, stomach, curled up on his side. Seated on the floor or in a chair.

(2) Vary the time from a few seconds to a minute or two.

(3) Have him stretch hard and long, then relax and rest again.

(4) Have him change from one position to another, resting in each position for a given time. Encourage slow controlled, differentiated movements as he changes positions. Ask him to move as quietly as possible.

2. Repetiton of same movements.

   a. Help the child to relax as he is seated Indian fashion on the floor or on a low stool. Then ask him to move rhythmically as he:

    (1) Raises and lowers his upper torso.

    (2) Rocks back and forth.

    (3) Rocks side to side.

    The child's buttocks should remain on the floor or stool. Only the upper part of the body is to move.

   b. As he is seated as above or in a chair also have him relax, then move a part or parts of himself, rhythmically. He should learn to move an arm, a leg or any part of the arm or leg—i.e., ankle, wrist, knee, elbow, fingers—in a variety of patterns singly and together.

    (1) Have the child use clap, tap, rub movements.

    (2) Have him push and pull objects across a surface, out and back and back and forth across in front of himself.

    (3) Encourage the child to "sing" as he moves, repeat single words or sounds rhythmically.

   c. Visual motor rhythms. Have the child rhythmically look and touch one target then another. Use two penlights or sound-making targets. Flash or sound one then the other, rhythmically. Vary the position of the targets so that the child will be required to move his hand and eyes in the following directions:

    (1) Up and down.

    (2) Near and far.

    (3) Side to side.

    Do not be concerned if he changes hands while performing.

   d. A variety of rhythms may be used but emphasis should be on the ones that are slow and relaxing:

    (1) Let each child take turns setting the rhythm, while the others follow.

    (2) Encourage each child to make rhythmic vocal sounds as he moves.

(3) Have the children perform as the teacher hums, chants in sing-song, i.e., up and down, up and down, and to music. String music is best. Do not use precussion at this time.

SEQUENTIAL MOVEMENTS

1. Have the child repeat a series of previously learned movements.
2. Have him combine previously learned movements and activities in imitation and symbolic games.
3. Encourage the sequential handling of objects (see "Preparation for Math," this section).

SYMBOLIC PLAY

Encourage the child to enter into games of dramatization. The games should be representative of the child's previous experiences at home, at school, in his immediate neighborhood or of one of the stories read to him.

At first you may get only simple one-activity performances such as pretending to sweep the floor, sleep, feed the baby or a pet, write (scribble), read a book, go to church or the store, walk like an animal, etc. Later the child will combine two or three such acts.

appendix a

Problems and Suspected Deficits

RELATIONSHIP OF PERCEPTUAL-MOTOR INTERFERENCES TO BEHAVIORAL AND EDUCATIONAL DEFICITS

Over the years, the teachers and parents with whom we have worked have observed and reported multiple signs or indicators of behavioral and learning deficits. Many of these parents endeavored to remediate the deficits, only to find that after hours and hours of drill, the deficit prevailed or a splinter skill had developed and that the learned task still was not integrated with previous learning.

Why? Because the parents had been observing the product or end result of the child's performance rather than the process he used to achieve the end result, and they proceeded to remediate that which they had observed. They failed and the child failed, for he was still using his old, inefficient process; with it, he could produce only minimal if any change in his work.

For clarification, let's look at an example.

John's writing is small, cramped, and poorly formed. He resists writing, puts it off, doesn't finish his written work, and daydreams instead. But keeping him in at recess and after school to finish his work has not improved his writing nor his work habits. Neither has sending his work home to be completed. However, presenting material that requires minimal writing has helped. He has become more attentive and his participation in class has improved, but his writing has not. Typing was introduced, but he had as much difficulty with it as he did in manipulating a pencil. Why? First, because the processes needed for writing and typing are balance, fine differentiation, coordination and control of the arms, hands, fingers and eyes, visual-motor match, and laterality and none of these have developed adequately in John.

The following charts have been included as an aid in identifying the processes that are inadequate plus other interfering factors, such as hyper- and hypo-tension, splinter skills, and techniques developed by the child as a means of avoiding repeated failure. The teaching of the basic processes is elaborated in the Pre-Readiness text.

Behavior

Problem	Suspected Deficits Or Interferences
Impulsive, irresistible reactions to stimuli.	Kinesthetic figure-ground. Movement control.
Daydreams.	Avoidance technique due to inability to trust environment.
Repetition of familiar task again and again.	Rigidity.
Failure to finish work.	Hypertension. Inadequate space and time organization.
Hypoactivity or lethargic action.	Inadequate kinesthetic figure-ground.
Hyperactivity.	Kinesthetic figure-ground. Movement control.
Difficulty in getting started on task.	Inadequate kinesthetic figure-ground. Initiation of movement.
Explosions into rage and attack although not normally aggressive.	Hypertension. Poor movement control.
Distractibility.	Inadequate visual balance. Hypertension or balance problem.
Inability to stay in one place.	Inadequate movement control. Hypertension or balance problem.
Significant variation in performance level from day to day or hour to hour.	Hypertension and/or difficulty with structure.
Clumsiness or awkwardness.	Poor differentiation or coordination control.
Nervous traits or mannerisms (bites nails, chews pencils).	Hypertension.
Inability to stand in line.	Inadequate movement control, balance, and/or space structure.
Resistance to change.	Rigidity.

161

Behavior

Problems	Suspected Deficits Or Interferences
Trouble maker in the classroom.	Avoidance technique due to inability to trust environment.
Insecurity; need for constant approval.	Inadequate body image. Perceptual discrimination.
Playing with older or younger children.	Avoidance technique to meet own needs.
Withdrawal. Shyness.	Rigidity. Avoidance technique to protect self from failure.
Grabbing, touching. Inability to wait turn.	Poor visual location, movement control, or visual-motor match. Hypertension.
Failure to enter into games.	Rigidity. Poor movement control, coordination, and/or balance. Inadequate space-time relationships.
Exaggerated emotional responses (laughs or talks too loud, etc.)	Hypertension. Poor breathing pattern.
Easy fatigue.	Inadequate visual coordination, visual-motor match, kinesthetic awareness. Hypertension.
Poor posture.	Hypertension or hypotension. Inadequate balance or coordination.
Ability to hear instructions and repeat them but inability to perform them.	Difficulty with movement initiation and/or auditory-motor translation.
Need to always be the leader, captain, director, etc.	Inadequate spatial-temporal organization. Technique to avoid failure.

Language

Problems	Suspected Deficits Or Interferences
Minimal language.	Hypertension. Inadequate movement control. Over-attention to movement. Inadequate auditory input or feedback.
Failure to intitate sounds or words.	Poor auditory figure-ground. Hyperkinesia interfering with attention to auditory input and/or movement of the speech mechanism.
Talking too fast and running words together.	Hypertension interfering with breathing. Poor rhythm and/or sequencing.
Poor pronunciation (lack of certain sounds):	Hypertension interfering with movement of speech mechanism.
Back sounds.	Hypertension in neck and jaw.
Front sounds.	Hypotension or hypertension in face and lips.
Capability of repetition but not of going on to development of language.	Hypertension. Poor motor development. Inadequate integrative learning. Words not related to anything.
Ability to talk fluently with good inflection but not understandably. (Child sounds as if he were speaking a foreign language.)	Development of an inner language but not a social language. Faulty sequencing. Poor auditory discrimination.
Speech is an effort; inability to speak without seeming to drag words out.	Difficulty differentiating. Hypertension. Inadequate breathing pattern.

163

Language

Problems	Suspected Deficits Or Interferences
Difficulty in recognizing differences in sounds or words presented orally.	Auditory discrimination problem due to hypertension or over visualization.
Difficulty in understanding oral instructions or directions.	Hypertension. Poor auditory reception. Integration problems.
Difficulty in expressing self verbally.	Hypertension. Inadequate sequencing. Poor integration.
Difficulty in sorting out similar words on an auditory basis.	Poor auditory discrimination due to hypertension. Overattention to movement, balance, hearing defect, etc.
Ability to see words and match them but inability to name them.	Difficulty with visual to vocal translation.
Imitation of words which become more and more distorted with use.	Difficulty with auditory feedback of own voice. Poor auditory-motor match.

Mathematics

Problems	Suspected Deficits Of Interferences
Difficulty counting objects using hand to point.	Hypertension. Inadequate movement control. Inadequate ocular control. Inadequate visual-motor match.
Difficulty counting objects using eyes only.	Inadequate ocular control. Hypertension.
Ability to memorize facts but not to relate information to groups or sets.	Inadequate visual space. Inadequate auditory to visual translation. Inadequate temporal to spatial translation.
Inability to get amount without counting out even small sets.	Poor visual space. Inadequate constructive form (i.e., has difficulty seeing parts to whole relationship).
Inability to keep problems organized on the page and/or to keep numbers organized in a problem.	Poor ocular control. Poor motor control. Poor visual-motor match. Inadequate space organization.
Inability to visualize numbers as representing groups or sets.	Inadequate ocular control. Inadequate visual-motor match. Inadequate visual space organization. Lack of visual imagery.
Reversal of numbers (31—13).	Inadequate laterality. Inadequate visual control and/or visual space structure.
Reversal of the vertical direction when working a problem: $\begin{array}{r} 12 \\ -\ 6 \\ \hline 14 \end{array}$	Inadequate vertical space structure. Inadequate visual control. Body verticality.
Reversal of the number heard.	Poor auditory directionality or sequencing. Poor auditory to visual translation.

Mathematics

Problems	Suspected Deficits Or Interferences
Inability to work story problems: Inability to read them. Ability to read but not to work them.	Diagnosis of the reading problem. Difficulty with temporal organization in space, sequencing, and ordering. Lack of comprehension.
Has none or only one definition for mathematical signs (i.e., "+" is "plus" but not "add to" or "and").	Poor teaching. Splinter skills or nonintegrative learning due to various faulty processes.
Confusion of the "+" and "-" signs or failure to be cognizant of change from one to another.	Hypertension. Poor ocular control.
Difficulty with concepts (i.e., does not see the relationships between addition and subtraction, addition and multiplication, etc.).	Memorization of perceptual facts rather than developmental learning.
Difficulty manipulating small objects for concrete math work.	Inadequate differentiation, coordination, and motor control.
Difficulty applying math to every-day life.	Memorized rather than generalized learning due to a combination of inadequate prereadiness and readiness processes.
Difficulty in making change; using units and tens blocks; seeing units, tens, and hundreds relationships in problems.	Difficulty with whole-part relationships due to a combination of inadequate prereadiness and readiness processes.

Physical Education

Problems	Suspected Deficits Or Interferences
Walking or Running	
Arms hang at sides.	Inadequate coordination of upper and lower body.
Arms move but are out of synchrony with legs.	Inadequate coordination of upper and lower body.
Arms move but are out of control.	Inadequate coordination of upper and lower body. Inadequate control and coordination of body parts.
Tumbling	
Poor flexibility (back and neck).	Hypertension. Inadequate coordination and control.
Stumbling and falling.	Inadequate time organization.
Stopping movement prior to mounting apparatus.	Inadequate space organization.
Difficulty with placement of arms and other body parts.	Poor body image.
Trampoline	
Arms move but do not really help.	Inadequate coordination of upper and lower body.
Restricted movement of legs and arms.	Inadequate coordination of sides.
Difficulty with back drop.	Inadequate space organization.
Timidity regarding drop on trampoline.	Inadequate space organization.
Eyes glued to feet.	Inadequate space organization.
Jumping too high.	Inadequate control.
Falling forward.	Tight heel cords. Hypertension.
Difficulty with sequencing tricks.	Poor time organization.

Physical Education

Problems	Suspected Deficits Or Interferences
Pool	
Fast movement only (sprinting).	Hypertension. Poor timing.
Fear of water.	Inadequate kinesthetic figure-ground, tactual, and kinesthetic space.
Anti-diving.	Fear of space.
Inability to change strokes.	Inability to pace. Poor motor organization. Stroke is a splinter skill.
Thrashing at water.	Inadequate movement control, balance, and space organization.
Foot and leg cramps.	Hypertension. Overuse of wrong muscle groups.
Lower-leg kick.	Poor hip differentiation. Poor kinesthetic awareness.
Anti-face in the water.	Overdependence on vision. Inadequate breathing patterns.
Locker room confusion.	Poor space organization.
General Gym	
Choosing one spot in which to move.	Limited space organization.
Imitating others.	Poor kinesthetic awareness.
Inability to follow instructions.	Difficulty integrating kinesthetic figure-ground with auditory input.

Reading

Problems	Suspected Deficits Or Interferences
Difficulty with left-to-right progression.	Inadequate directionality.
Slumping in chair.	Poor balance.
Leaning on desk.	Hypertension.
Covering one eye or tilting head too far right or left.	Inadequate visual coordination.
Turning head back and forth as he reads.	Eyes not differentiated from head. Eyes locked together rather than coordinated.
Shifting book. Fixating eyes on one area and keeping reading material in that one area.	Inadequate motor and ocular differentiation, coordination, and/or directionality.
Skipping words, phrases, and lines.	Lack of ocular control. Hypertension. Poor rhythm or sequencing.
Skipping back and forth within a line.	Inadequate ocular control. Hypertension.
Word omissions and substitutions.	Inadequate ocular control.
Reversals of letters or words.	Inadequate laterality and directionality.
Difficulty with word recognition.	Poor ocular control. Lack of constructive form.
Difficulty in breaking words into phonetic sounds.	Inadequate constructive form.
Difficulty in blending phonetic sounds into words.	Inadequate auditory and/or visual constructive form (i.e., does not see or hear the relationship between the parts and the whole).
Running words together (e.g., "this is on" read as "this son"). Attaching letters of next word on the word (e.g., "many can stop" read as "many cans top")	Inadequate visual control. Poor visual figure-ground. Faulty special organization.
Reading words haltingly, one at a time.	Hypertension. Inadequate ocular or breathing control.

Reading

Problems	Suspected Deficits Or Interferences
Reversals of word order.	Inadequate ocular control. Difficulty in sequencing.
Failure to see letters in proper order in a word (i.e., says "stop" for "spot").	Inadequate from constancy. Poor ocular control.
Good reading ability but poor comprehension.	Hypertension. Poor ocular control. Child works so hard to read that he cannot attend to content.

Writing

Problems	Suspected Deficits Or Interferences
Small, cramped writing.	Hypertension. Inadequate differentation, co-ordination, and/or movement control. Inadequate space structure.
Eyes placed very close to work. Eyes and sometimes head move with every movement of the pencil.	Inadequate visual-motor match.
Letters all the same height. No extension above or below.	Poor range of movement due to overcontrol or hyperten-sion. Inadequate body verticality. Inadequate vertical space.
Letter reversals or frequent hesitations.	Inadequate laterality and/or directionality.
Rapid writing running letters and words together.	Inadequate movement con-trol, timing, visual-motor match, or space organization.
Writing slanted up or down. Difficulty in getting started in writing. Inadequate spacing.	Inadequate visual-motor match and/or space organi-zation.
Difficulty in copying. Losing place while writing. Looking back and forth repeatedly while writing.	Inadequate ocular control. Inadequate temporal to spatial translation.
Avoidance or dislike of writing. Failure to finish work.	Inadequate differentiation, coordination, control, visual-motor match, etc. Hypo- or hypertension.
Jumbling of letters in a word even though oral spelling is adequate.	Inability to sequence visually. Inadequate visual-motor match which interferes with sequencing.
Failure to hold paper with nonwriting hand.	Inadequate differentiation, lateral coordination. Poor balance. Hypertension.

Writing

Problems	Suspected Deficits Or Interferences
Difficulty in forming letters.	Inadequate laterality and directionality. Inadequate form perception, visual figure-ground, and/or visual to motor translation.
Ability to copy but inability to write from memory.	Inadequate integration.

appendix b

Developmental Checklist

Use of the following Checklist will help to develop awareness of the processes that a child should have if he is to learn adequately.

Almost any of the tests or measures used to assess a child's developmental and learning abilities (i.e., the *Purdue Perceptual Motor Survey, ITPA, Frostig, WISC, SAT,* or *SRA*) can supply the necessary information if the observer takes the time to study how the child performs and why he performs as he does. The examiner must not look just at the product of the child's efforts.

As the child develops the various processes, his accomplishments can be indicated on the Checklist and, thus, at a glance, the teacher or therapist can determine the child's progress plus present and future needs.

CHECKLIST I

Body Parts and Movement

Differentiation:	
Movement Figure-Ground	
Isolation of Muscles	
Movement Control:	
Initiation	
Termination	
Over Time	
Automatic Movement	
Coordination:	
All parts of:	
Arms	
Legs	
Speech Mechanism	
Limbs:	
Bilateral	
Unilateral	
Cross-Lateral	
Contrast	
Apply to All of Above:	
Synchronize	
Alternate	
Cross Midline	
Sequence	
All Four Quadrants	
Motor Problem-Solving	
Using Body Parts	
Total Body	
Behavior	
Structure:	
Child	
Task	
Environment	
Rules	

Ocular-Visual-Motor

Ocular Movements:	
Peripheral Awareness	
Central Fixations:	
Each Eye	
Both Eyes	
Convergence	
Search	
Visual-Motor Match:	
Hand-Eye	
Eye-Hand	
Visual Monitoring	

Motor-Perceptual Generalizations

Balance:	
Static:	
Seated	
Hands and Knees	
Kneeling	
Standing	
Dynamic:	
Seated	
Hands and Knees	
Kneeling	
Standing	
Contact:	
Reach	
Grasp	
Release	
Locomotion:	
Quadruped:	
Crawl (on Stomach)	
Creep	
Climb	
Biped:	
Walk	
Jump	
Hop	
Skip	
Receipt and Propulsion:	
Bilateral	
Unilateral:	
Give and Take	
Take and Place	
Roll	
Throw	
Catch	
Push	
Pull	
Bat or Strike	

Motor-Perceptual:
Attention:
Kinesthetic Attention
Tactual Attention
Visual Attention
Auditory Attention
Match:
Tactual to Kinesthetic
Visual to Kinesthetic
Auditory to Kinesthetic
Vocal to Kinesthetic
Visual-Auditory to Kinesthetic
Auditory-Vocal to Kinesthetic
Exploration:
Tactual-Kinesthetic
Visual-Kinesthetic
Auditory-Kinesthetic
Vocal-Auditory
Visual-Auditory-Kinesthetic
Visual-Auditory-Kinesthetic
Translation:
Visual Kinesthetic
Auditory Kinesthetic
Visual Vocal
Auditory Vocal
Generalization
Perceptual:
Associations:
Visual-Visual
Auditory-Auditory
Visual-Auditory
Auditory-Visual
Auditory-Vocal-Visual
Generalization

Perceptual-Motor

Body Image:

Body form:

Location of parts:

Kinesthetic

Visual

Identification of parts:

Kinesthetic

Tactual

Visual

Body Space

Orientation:

  Egocentric:

    Body Part to Whole

    Part to Part

  Subjective:

    Self to Object

    Object to Self

Body Time

Movement vs. Nonmovement:

Duration:

  Continuity

  Repetition

Synchronous Movements

Rhythmic Movement

Sequential Movement

appendix c

The Lesson Plan

The lesson plan supplies spaces for: recording tasks recommended, procedures for performance of tasks, and comments regarding the outcome of the tasks.

In the first column, the evaluator lists the recommended tasks and the number of the page in which they occur in the curriculum.

The column headed "Procedures" should be used to describe in as much detail as possible how the task is to be performed, number of times or time allotted for it, and so on.

The last column should be used by the person working with the child to comment upon the outcome of the task. What happened? If performance was good, why was it good? If poor, why? The back of the sheet may be used for additional observations and suggestions.

Again, we wish to stress the importance of well-kept lesson plans. They supply on-going records of the tasks tried, time involved, successes, detours, and failures.

LESSON PLAN

Date_____

Diagnostician_____

Child's Name_____

Teacher or
Therapist_____

Task	Procedure	Comments, Suggestions, Questions

appendix d

Projection Charts

The Initial Evaluation Projection Chart is designed to keep a record of the child's learning interferences and the remediation goals.

In the first column, list the presenting problems or the reasons given for referral.

In the second column, record the deficits and/or interferences noted during the evaluation and checked on the Developmental Check List.

Under Short-Term Goals, list those deficits or interferences that are to receive immediate attention and remediation. In the narrow column next to it, give the estimated length of time required for remediation.

Under Intermediate Goals, list the the processes that are to be remediated after the short-term goals have been accomplished; again, estimate the length of time remediation should require.

The last columns are for the final goals, those accomplishments which are seen as the ultimate achievements that will permit the child to enter into and become a comfortable and useful part of his environment, and the estimated time for remediation.

The Re-Evaluation Projection Chart is to be used as an extension of the Initial Chart. It supplies spaces to record goals achieved as well as projected goals.

INITIAL EVALUATION PROJECTION CHART

Child's Name _____

Birthdate _____

Diagnostician _____

Date _____

Presenting Problems	Deficits and Interferences	Immediate Goals	Am't of Time	Intermediate Goals	Am't of Time	Ultimate Goals	Am't of Time

RE-EVALUATION PROJECTION CHART

Child's Name _____   Diagnostician _____

Birthdate _____   Date _____

Goals Achieved	Immediate Goals	Am't of Time	Intermediate Goals	Am't of Time	Ultimate Goals	Am't of Time

appendix e

Glossary

Alternating Movements: Movements changing successively or in turns; thus, the child makes a movement, then a second movement, then back to the first movement, and so on. (For example, swinging an arm back and forth or moving first one arm and then the other.)

Balance and Posture: A motor generalization which gives the child a stable orientation to gravity and permits him to move flexibly without its loss.

Behavior Control: The ability to control one's actions.

Bilateral: The use of both sides of the body in a simultaneous and parallel manner.

Cephalo-Caudal: Development beginning in the head-neck region and proceeding down through the body.

Concept: The abstract manipulation, organization, and integration of relationships among percepts.

Contrasting Movements: Movements which oppose each other. (For example, one arm moves in as the other moves out.)

Convergence: The coordinated turning of the eyes inward to focus on a certain point.

Crossing the Midline: The Midline is the center of a child's body, the zero point of origin for the infant's movements. The crossing of the midline is movement across that point.

Dynamic Balance: Maximum balancing adjustments of the body during movement.

Eye-Hand Cordination: Controlled and matched movement of the hand and eye working in unison.

Fine Motor: Tasks that require the use of fine motor systems; that is, muscles required in speaking, eye movements, use of hands, etc.

Generalization: Organization of similar but not identical patterns.

Gross Motor: Activities that require the use of groups of large muscles for movement, such as, creeping, reaching, kicking, etc.

Halo: A larger area surrounding the deficit, a pseudo-deficit built as a protection against failure.

Hypertension: The firing of more motor energy then needed to perform.

Kinesthesis: Awareness of presence, position, or movement due to stimulation of sensory nerve endings in muscles, joints, and tendons.

Laterality: The inner awareness of the difference between the two sides of the body.

Learning Disability: Any interference with learning.

Locomotion: Motor patterns which permit purposeful movement of the body.

Locomotor Pattern: Any patterned form of locomotion, such as, walking, running, jumping, hopping, skipping, galloping, and crawling.

Motor Development: The differentiation of movements and the integration of reflexes.

Motor Differentiation: The process of sorting out and activation of muscle groups in patterns following the cephalo-caudal and proximo-distal development.

Movement Control: The ability to move and control body parts.

Movement Patterns: The organization of movements into patterns so that the child can interact with the environment with control and purpose.

Perceptual Process: The continuous reorganization of sensory elements in relation to past and on-going experiences; the integration of this information into a total form with an emergant quality or qualities.

Peripheral Vision: Visual sensations arising from the visual sense cells lying outside the central (foveal) area of the retina.

Proximo-Distal: The direction from the center outward. Movements of large muscle groups lying toward the center of the body extremities. Thus, movements of the total arm precede those of the wrist and fingers.

Receipt and Propulsion: Activities involving experiences with movements toward and away from the child.

Relax: To make or become less tense or rigid.

Rhythm: An activity repeated in time at equal temporal intervals. It encompasses kinesthesia, vision, and audition.

Rigidity: Inflexibility, undeviation.

Space Structure: The localization in the environment of many objects simultaneously and the preservation of the relationship between them and the organism.

Splinter Skill: Isolated and specific learning, out of context, in order to satisfy the demands of a specific task. For example, memorization of $2 + 2 = 4$ without understanding of what the symbols stand for, drawing of a form through the use of a series of marks with fingers that are not yet differentiated.

Synchrony: Occurring simultaneously.

Tactual Awareness: A broad range of touch sensations, including textures, being touched, and localization and identification of these points of contact. Tactual information by itself furnishes limited data unless accompanied by movement which is essential for the continuation of the stimulus.

Tactual-Kinesthetic: The coordination of tactual and kinesthetic information which furnishes continuity or wholeness to a stimulus. Tactual-kinesthetic learning (awareness) is necessary to the development of relationships and comparisons.

Tension: (Body): Physiological tension caused by factors within the child as opposed to environmentally related tension, externally caused by such sources as anxiety about an exam, etc. While environmental tension may add to the physiological tension, it is not the basic cause. These internal causes are most often caused by inadequate body differentiation, coordination, inadequate ocular coordination, control, etc. Research is beginning to indicate that allergies, chronic illness, and chemical imbalance within the child are also factors.

Visual Monitoring: Visual checking of movement responses which permit the child to perform with accuracy and to correct errors immediately and spontaneously.

appendix f

General References

Alfred I. Dupont Special School District. *Graphic Readiness.* Wilmington, Delaware: Project Child, ESEA, Title III, 1968.

Almy, M.; Chittendon, E; and Miller, P. *Young Children's Thinking.* New York: Columbia University Teachers College Press, 1967.

Arena, J.I. *Teaching through Sensory-Motor Experiences.* San Rafael, California: Academic Therapy Publications, 1969.

Bereiter, C. *Arithmetic and Mathematics.* San Rafael, California: Dimensions Publishing Co., 1968.

Bush, W.J., and Giles, M.T. *Aids to Psycholinguistic Teaching.* Columbus, Ohio: Charles E. Merrill Publishing Co., 1969.

Chaney, C.M., and Kephart, N.C. *Motoric Aids to Perceptual Training.* Columbus, Ohio: Charles E. Merrill Publishing Co., 1968.

Church, J., editor. *Three Babies.* New York: Random House, 1966.

Engelmann, S. *Conceptual Learning.* San Rafael, California: Dimensions Publishing Co., 1969.

Fiorentino, M.R. *Normal and Abnormal Development.* Springfield, Illinois: Charles C. Thomas Publishing Co., 1972.

_____. *Reflex Testing Methods for Evaluating CNS Development.* Springfield, Illinois: Charles C. Thomas Publishing Co., 1968.

Flavell, J. *The Developmental Psychology of Jean Piaget.* New York: Van Nostrand Reinhold, 1963.

Frostig, M. *Frostig Program.* Chicago: The Follett Publishing Co., 1964.

Frymier, J.R. *The Nature of Educational Method.* Columbus, Ohio: Charles E. Merrill Publishing Co., 1965.

Gardner, M.D. *The Principles of Exercise Therapy.* London: G. Belle & Sons, 1960.

Gattegno, C. *Arithmetic—A Teacher's Introduction to Cuisenaire-Gattegno Methods.* New York: Cusenaire of America, 1960.

Gessell, A. *The First Five Years of Life.* New York: Harper & Row, 1940.

Haeussermann, E. *Developmental Potential of Preschool Children.* New York Grune & Stratton, 1958.

Harmon, D.B. *Optometric Extension Program.* Duncan, Oklahoma: Post Graduate Courses, 1969.

Hellmuth, J., Jr., editor. *Learning Disorders,* volume 1. Seattle, Washington: Special Child Publications, 1965.

Holt, J. *How Children Learn.* New York: Pitman Publishing Co., 1967.

Hughes, L. *The First Book of Rhythms.* New York: Franklin Watts, 1954.

Illingsworth, R.S. *The Development of the Infant and Young Child: Normal and Abnormal.* Baltimore, Maryland: Williams & Wilkins Co., 1970.

Jacobson, E. *Progressive Relaxation.* Chicago: University of Chicago Press, 1938.

Johnson, D. J., and Myklebust, H. R. *Learning Disabilities: Educational Principles and Practice.* New York: Grune & Stratton, 1967.

Karnes, M.B. *Helping Young Children Develop Language Skills.* Arlington, Virginia: Council for Exceptional Children, 1968.

Kellogg, R. *Analyzing Children's Art.* Palo Alto, California: National Press Books, 1969.

_____. *What Children Scribble and Why.* Palo Alto, California: National Press Books, 1959.

Kephart, N.C. *Learning Disability: An Educational Adventure.* West Lafayette, Indiana: Kappa Delta Pi Press, 1968.

_____. *The Slow Learner in the Classroom,* 2d ed. Columbus, Ohio: Charles E. Merrill Publishing Co., 1971.

Kephart, N.C., and Roach, E.G. *The Purdue Perceptual-Motor Survey.* Columbus, Ohio: Charles E. Merrill Publishing Co., 1968.

Kephart, N.C.; Ebersole, M.; and Ebersole, J. *Steps to Achievement for the Slow Learner.* Columbus, Ohio: Charles E. Merrill Publishing Co., 1968.

Kinsley, B. *Reading Skills.* San Francisco: Fearon Publishers, 1968.

Lovell, K. *The Growth of Basic Mathematical and Scientific Concepts in Children.* London: University of London Press, 1961.

Lowenfeld, V., and Brittain, W.L. *Creative and Mental Growth.* New York: The Macmillan Co., 1965.

Maier, H.W. *Three Theories of Child Development.* New York: Harper & Row, 1965.

Montgomery, C. *Art for Teachers of Children,* 2d ed. Columbus, Ohio: Charles E. Merrill Publishing Co., 1973.

Montessori, M. *Dr. Montessori's Own Handbook.* New York: Schocken Books, 1965.

————. *The Montessori Method.* New York: Schocken Books, 1964.

Patterson, G.R., and Patterson, M.E. *Living with Children.* Champaign, Illinois: Research Press Co., 1970.

Phillips, J.C., Jr. *The Origins of Intellect: Piaget's Theory.* San Francisco: W.H. Freeman Co., 1969.

Piaget, J. *The Origins of Intelligence in Children.* New York: W.W. Norton & Co., 1963.

————. *Six Psychological Studies.* New York: Random House, 1967.

Pitcher, E.G.; Lasher, M.G.; Feinburg, S.G.; and Braun, N.A. *Helping Young Children Learn,* 2d ed. Columbus, Ohio: Charles E. Merrill Publishing Co., 1974.

Prudden, B. *How to Keep Your Child Fit from Birth to Six.* New York: Harper & Row, 1964.

Smith, J.M., and Smith, D.E.P. *Child Management.* Ann Arbor, Michigan: Ann Arbor Publishers, 1969.

Strauss, A.A., and Kephart, N.C. *Psychopathology and Education of the Brain-Injured Child.* New York: Grune & Stratton, 1955.

Vereecken, P. *Spatial Development.* Groningen: J.B. Wolters, 1961.

Young, E., and Hawks, S. *Moto-Kinesthetic Speech Training.* Palo Alto, California: Stanford University Press, 1938.

Zimmerman, I.L.; Steiner, V.G.; and Evatt, R.L. *Preschool Language Scale.* Columbus, Ohio: Charles E. Merrill Publishing Co., 1969.